AF228238

Building Simply

Building Simply

A guideline

Florian Nagler (ed.)

Birkhäuser
Basel

Concept: Prof. Dipl.-Ing. Florian Nagler, TUM – Lehrstuhl für Entwerfen und Konstruieren

Contributors: Dipl.-Ing. (FH) Architekt Tilmann Jarmer, M.A. (TUM); Dipl.-Ing. Architektin Anne Niemann; Laura Franke, M.Sc.; Laura Traub, B.A. (TUM); Johannes Sack, M.Sc.; Zsofia Varga, M.Sc.; Dipl.-Ing. Stephan Ott, M.A.; Fabian Diewald, M.Sc.; Dipl.-Ing. (Univ.) Alexander Knirsch; Prof. Dipl.-Ing. Thomas Auer; Prof. Dr.-Ing. Christoph Gehlen; Prof. Dr.-Ing. Stefan Winter

Photographs: Sebastian Schels; Tilmann Jarmer (S. 52, 86, 88); Max Kratzer (S. 5); Laura Franke (S. 2)

Translation from German into English: Raymond Peat
Copy editing: Keonaona Peterson
Project management: Alexander Felix, Regina Herr
Production: Heike Strempel
Layout and cover design: Floyd Schulz
Typesetting: Laura Traub, Heike Strempel
Paper: 120 g/m² Tauro Offset
Printing: Optimal media GmbH, Röbel/Müritz
Image Editing: pixelstorm, Vienna

Library of Congress Control Number: 2021945355

Bibliographic information published by the German National Library
The German National Library lists this publication in the Deutsche Nationalbibliografie; detailed bibliographic data are available on the Internet at http://dnb.dnb.de.

ISBN 978-3-0356-2464-9
e-ISBN (PDF) 978-3-0356-2466-3
German Print-ISBN 978-3-0356-2463-2

© 2022 Birkhäuser Verlag GmbH, Basel
P.O. Box 44, 4009 Basel, Switzerland
Part of Walter de Gruyter GmbH, Berlin/Boston

9 8 7 6 5 4 3 2 1   www.birkhauser.com

Content

Foreword

No one just gets up one morning and suddenly decides they would like to build more simply in the future. While that's true, after twenty years of building practice and constantly striving to develop projects that make sense energetically and in which we use our resources responsibly, I had become seriously concerned about the increasing complexity in construction, both with respect to the types of construction adopted and the ever-more-intensive use of technology. The very ambitious Schmuttertal secondary school project in Diedorf near Augsburg, which we designed and built together with Hermann Kaufmann Architekten, impressively brought home to me this increasing complexity and its associated problems. On the one hand, the school, which has won several awards as a timber structure, a plus-energy school, and a secondary school with an innovative educational concept, is an exemplary project that we developed and built together with the German Federal Environmental Foundation (DBU) as part of a research project for the district of Augsburg. On the other hand, the fact that it took three years of monitoring to adjust the building services systems—or as someone more aptly put it, "to get them running"—really worried me. Not to mention all the effort that went into the design of the highly complex building itself, which was optimized to fulfill a wide range of functional requirements and is multilayered in the truest sense of the word. After completion of the project, critically considering my own role left me with the impression that I had reached a dead end. I did not want to go on like this, creating buildings that make such extreme demands on us in their design, on the contractor in their construction, and on the owner in their operation.

Inspired by examples of colleagues who had been through similar pain and were now looking for alternatives, such as those realized in Baumschlager Eberle's Building 2226 in Lustenau, we thought it was the right time to initiate a research project at the Technical University of Munich to investigate whether we might return to building more simply than we have generally done of late, in short: simple building. We were particularly interested in the question of whether the only response to the demands of our time was more and increasingly complex technology. The aim of the research project was to establish the principles upon which simple, robust buildings could be designed and their complexity reduced by, for example, using only single-skin, monolithic, or monomaterial construction. To ensure our investigations would be as relevant as possible, we selected the three most common materials used in building construction today and made them the focus of the research project: timber, concrete, and clay. Based on the multistage research project, which was funded by the Zukunft Bau research initiative and on which we have been working together with our colleagues at the Technical University of Munich since 2016, the B&O Group as the client then allowed us to build three "proper" research houses in Bad Aibling. The houses are now occupied and will be the subject of intense monitoring over the next two years.

This guide clearly and concisely summarizes the many considerations and previous findings from the research project and the subsequent related building projects. It is intended to inspire not only interested colleagues, but also building owners, craftsmen, and everyone involved in building to think about whether we can achieve beautiful, habitable houses by adopting somewhat reduced requirements and simpler but more robust means, yet still fulfill our responsibility for the sustainability of the built environment by consuming only a reasonable amount of energy and resources.

8

However, we should not be allowed to leave it at that. I have the impression that we have pushed open the door to further meaningful development with the findings from these research projects and revealed a broadening field upon which much more work deserves to be done. Consideration must also be given to reducing the amount of land used in all construction works in both urban and rural areas, utilizing existing buildings as a source of space and materials, and using materials that consume as little gray energy as possible, are easy to recycle, or can be returned to the cycle of nature. This will succeed only if all these aspects are considered from the earliest stages of the design process and if we as architects concern ourselves with the technical and construction aspects of our housing as well as its architectural potential. For example, deriving the shape of a window from the structural characteristics of the material is something that not only makes complete sense but is also a source of pleasure, in that the material creates an aesthetic of its own. This shift toward reducing the complexity of construction and technical systems also allows scope for revisiting architecture and engineering solutions for elements such as walls, ceilings, doors, windows, deep reveals, canopies, etc., with a proven record of success over centuries, which in turn allows us to work within the context of regional climates and building traditions.

In the meantime, we are striving to make use of the knowledge and experience gained from the research in almost any project. One thing we have learned along the way is that "simple building" means different things to different people. Some building craftsmen's organizations, for example, see simplicity as sticking exactly to the rules of the trade instead of questioning whether it could be done more simply. In architects' offices as well, it is much simpler and easier to reach for the book of approved details for a solution to any application than to develop an in-house "simple" detail. Perhaps the most important idea to grasp is that in order to build simply, architects and engineers must design simply. However, I do not see this as restrictive but as providing potential for future development. I am firmly convinced that dealing with all these concerns will not only make a contribution to the future conscious and careful use of the available resources but also to finding a contemporary architectural expression.

Florian Nagler, Munich, May 2021

A   Building Simply

The requirements relating to the fire safety and the thermal and sound insulation of build-ings have been continually rising for decades. The increased use of technical equipment and improvements to building materials will help the industry achieve the following high goals: to save energy (in the form of heat energy) and ensure building users can enjoy year-round comfort. As a result, technical equipment costs have formed an increasing proportion of total building costs over recent years. The German federal government established the Baukostensenkungskommission (BKSK), a commission to investigate reducing building costs. The commission identified Cost Group (CG) 400, which includes building services and other technical equipment, as being chiefly responsible for the rising cost of construction (Figure 1).

This has led to a multitude of regulations and technical rules that often overwhelm building designers and owners. The consequences of this are mistakes in planning, design, construction, and operation. "The things we design and subsequently construct are usually too complicated," concludes Florian Nagler, head of the research project Simple Building at the Technical University of Munich (TUM). "Therefore it is quite natural to ask: How could it be made simpler?" [2]

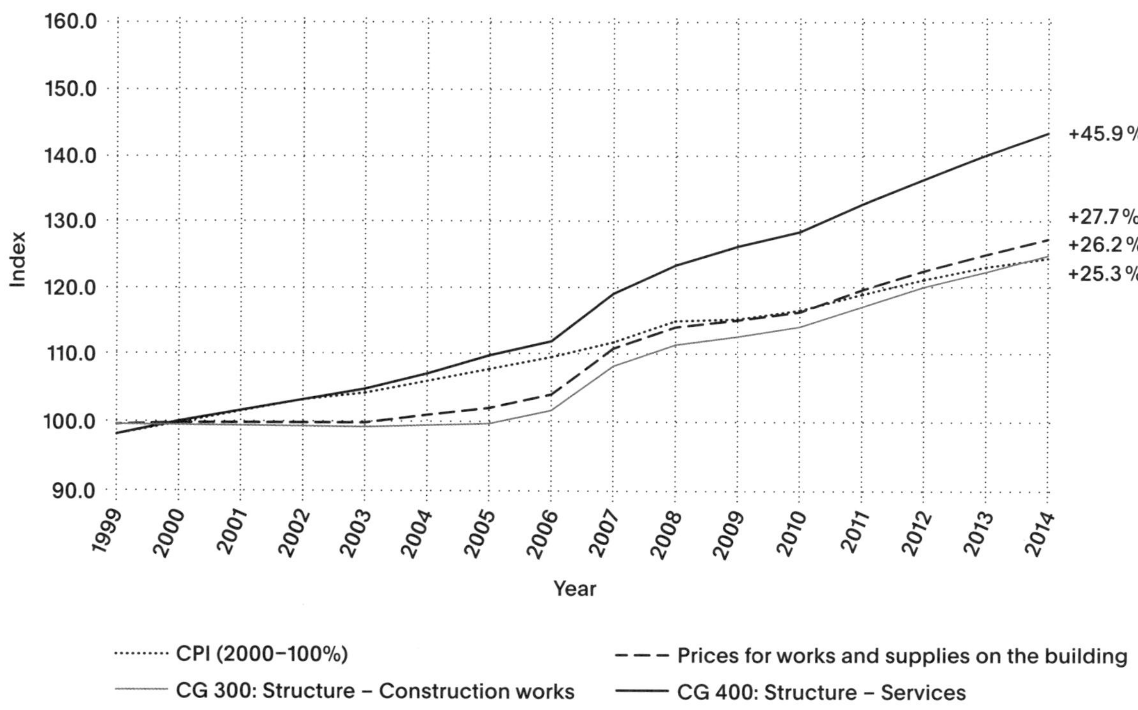

1
Graph of index series

"CG 300 – Structure – Construction works" and "CG 400 – Structure – Services" compared to the consumer price index (CPI) [1]

The Munich urban housing company GEWOFAG used a new project with six identically constructed residential buildings to compare different methods of saving energy. The analysis of the measurements revealed the following astonishing results: the actual energy savings did not come up to the theoretical calculated values [3]. One building, for example, had been particularly well insulated. Instead of the calculated 7 percent savings compared to the reference building, only 1 percent was recorded.

The deviation shown by the building with a ventilation system was even greater. Instead of the calculated 30 percent, an energy savings of only 7 percent was measured for the heating. If the electrical power for the ventilation is included in the figures, the primary energy demand is even higher than for a building without a ventilation system.

One measure was able to show a significant effect: in the case of one building, the windows are linked to the radiator valves. When a window is opened, the heating is switched off. Closing the window causes the heating to work normally again. This saved 23 percent of the heat energy. Unfortunately, not all residents saw this form of regulation as beneficial.

Is the solution to induce building users to behave in an energy-saving manner? An article entitled "Störfaktor Mensch" ("People: the disruptive factor") in a German news magazine discussed the GEWOFAG study [4]. The article cited "life factors" as the reason why the tested systems could not achieve the previously calculated savings when they were operating in real life. Against this backdrop, the number of standards applying to the building sector continues to rise. The article calculates that the number of standards rose from 5,000 to 20,000 between 1990 and 2016, which represents an increase of 300 percent. Many publications show that, although complexity increased, the intended energy efficiency during the building operation phase is achieved only after a phase of adjustment, if at all. As this type of monitoring is not performed on most buildings, it is fair to assume that most new buildings consume much more energy than is required.

Building 2226, an office building in Lustenau, Austria, designed by architects Baumschlager Eberle, points to a way out of this situation. In addition to having no heating, the building lacks a ventilation system and solar screening. Despite this, the temperature in the rooms remains a pleasant 22 to 26°C, from which the building gained its name. The rooms are heated solely by the energy sources within them such as people, equipment, and lighting. However, Project 2226 does not dispense totally with technology: the supply of fresh air is regulated by indoor sensors. The windows are opened automatically, depending on room temperature or the CO_2 content of the room's air. If they need to, building users can bypass the system and open individual windows by hand. Project 2226 demonstrates that architecture can be used to achieve results that contemporary popular opinion believes are possible only through the use of "a lot of technology" [5].

How can walls, ceilings, and windows be designed and arranged so as to be particularly advantageous in counteracting the cooling of rooms in winter and their overheating in summer? What role do people and the climate play in this?

The Simple Building Research Project

With these considerations in mind, the Technical University of Munich (TUM) adopted the topic of simple building as the focus of one of its research projects. The team of architects and engineers from the fields of construction and the environment, under the leadership of Prof. Florian Nagler, sought to answer the question of how architecture could be optimized by constructional means so that it requires the least possible technology to create a pleasant indoor climate. Something else they looked into was how these "simply built" buildings would perform compared to both standard and low-energy residential buildings with respect to their effects on the environment (see Infobox) and to their life cycle cost over a period of observation of 100 years. The research project Einfach Bauen—Integrale Strategien für energieeffizientes, einfaches Bauen mit Holz, Leichtbeton und hochwärmedämmendem Mauerwerk—Untersuchung der Wechselwirkungen von Raum, Konstruktion und Gebäudetechnik (Simple Building—Integral Strategies for Energy-Efficient Simple Building with Timber, Lightweight Concrete and Highly Insulating Masonry—investigation of the Interactions of Indoor Space, Design & Construction, and Building Services), funded through the research initiative Zukunft Bau (Future Building) [6], studied the fundamental principles of simple building over a period of two years.

2
Building 2226, designed by Austrian architects Baumschlager Eberle served as the reference building for the *Building Simply* research project

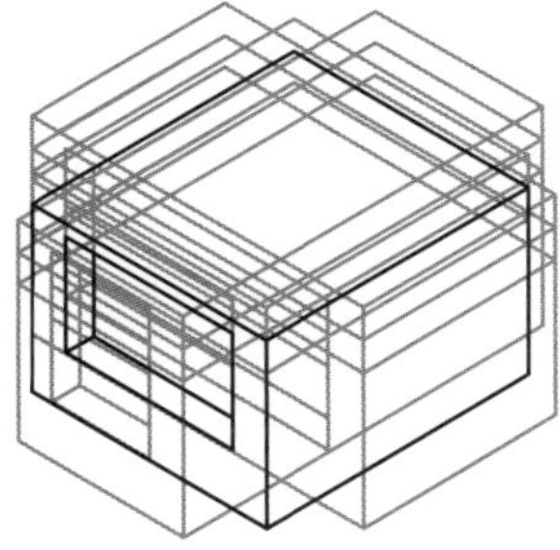

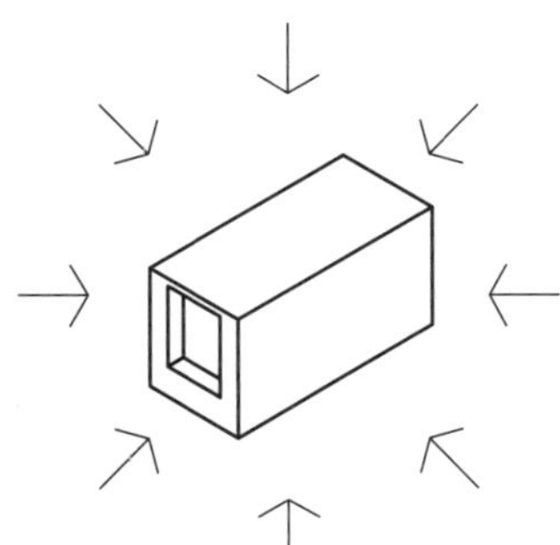

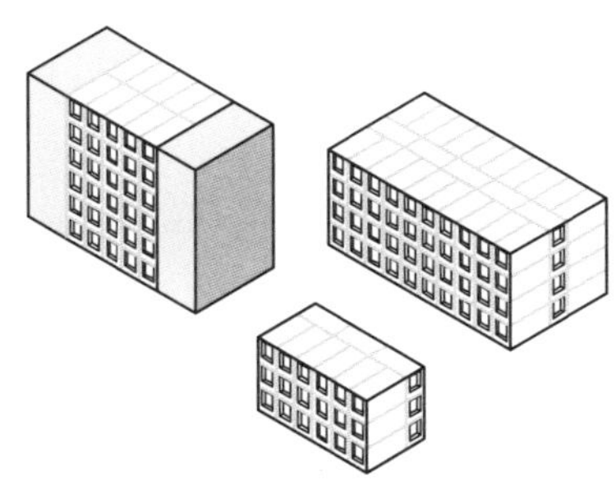

The team simulated and evaluated more than 2,000 different room variants with various proportions, window sizes, and materials. In a next step, the successful room configurations were investigated for their robustness against changing boundary conditions, for example, climate or user behavior. In the third and final step, schematic versions of three typical building forms of multiple-story residential buildings were created based on the above room variants for calculating quantities and estimating the energy consumption figures. Using full-scale models of the facades in solid timber, masonry, and insulating concrete, the researchers tested monolithic constructions incorporating simple functional details.

Taken overall, the results confirmed the initial proposed hypothesis that simple residential buildings with high-quality architecture fit for the purpose, robust construction, and reduced building technical services are superior to both standard and low-energy residential buildings with respect to their effects on the environment and life cycle costs. Simple building means designing a building to be robust and durable through a series of decisions from the very start of its planning.

The results can be found in the research report [6] and at *www.einfach-bauen.net.*

13   3
Sequence of work steps in the
Building Simply research project

Research Houses

In parallel to the theoretical work, the B&O Group, in cooperation with the research team, implemented the simple building strategy in three research houses in solid wood, thermally insulating masonry, and lightweight concrete. Three three-story residential buildings incorporating a total of twenty-three apartments were built without basements in Bad Aibling. The material and climate-conscious design for the buildings called for them to require minimal heat energy and not to overheat in summer. The use of single-layer components made from natural and renewable raw materials protects the environment over the whole life cycle of the building. The result is residential buildings that are simple to build and simple to operate. Long-term measurements can now check whether the theoretically derived performance matches that achieved in practice.

The guide in Part B explains the principles of simple building using examples drawn from the research houses.

Part C documents the buildings with drawings, photos, and parameters.

4
Facade models (1:1) for validating
the constructions

15

5
**View of the street with the
three research houses under
construction**

Simple building means…

- Reducing complexity in building construction. As early as the preliminary design stage, architecture can be used to create a building that intrinsically requires very little heat energy and does not overheat in summer. This enables the necessary building technical services to be reduced to a few robust systems.

- Using single-layer building components made from renewable or mineral raw materials where possible and taking their material properties into account to design robust and durable structures.

- Keeping the technical systems and the activities of the various trades employed on-site as cleanly separated from one another as possible. This simplifies the construction process enormously and minimizes demolition in the future when alterations to the building are made.

- Doing nothing that adversely affects the environment over the whole life cycle of the building. The result should be a building that is simple to build and simple to use.

Building Simply

Environmental Effect of Building—
Life Cycle Assessment

Environmentally compatible building means protecting the climate and the environment. This includes low material consumption, being careful with resources, and using environmentally friendly raw materials and secondary materials. Structures are used over a particularly long time, therefore their service life also needs to be correspondingly long and their construction durable. In addition, the building must be constructed such that its materials can be recycled on demolition and fed back into the material cycle [7].

Environmental Effects of Building

Greenhouse gases contribute to warming of Earth's atmosphere. One indicator for climate change is global warming potential (GWP) [8]. Greenhouse gas (GHG) emissions are expressed as their carbon dioxide equivalent (CO_2e) [9]. The impact the manufacture of a construction product has on climate change can be determined in a life cycle assessment (LCA). By adopting this approach, the environmental impact of the construction product or building can be improved or its environmental impact minimized.

Figure 6 compares a transatlantic flight with the three external wall variants from the research project Simple Building. The values for the external walls were calculated based on the usable floor area of a single-person household with an average floor area of 30 m².

Using the GWP value, it is possible, for example, to estimate the CO_2 emissions per square meter of external wall area of a single-person household over a total service life of 100 years for each of the different building types. Compared to a round-trip flight across the Atlantic, the figures for the buildings were 1.8 to 2.7 times greater. Three transatlantic flights would exceed the carbon dioxide equivalent of the external walls [10]. The transatlantic flight of one person for the purposes of this comparison was taken as a round trip from Frankfurt am Main to New York (12,374 km) [11] (Figure 6).

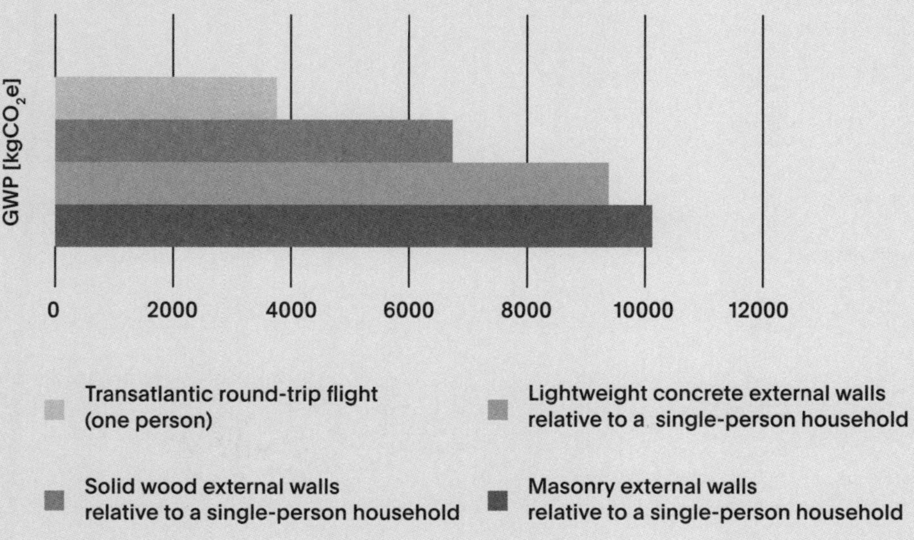

17

6
Comparison of GWP of the external walls of the research houses related to the usable area of a single-person household and a transatlantic flight for one person [12]

Life Cycle Assessment of Buildings

Environmentally compatible manufacturing processes can be identified using life cycle assessment. This represents a further step in the direction of climate and environment protection.

A life cycle assessment considers the environmental impacts of a product over its life cycle. These environmental impacts are the emissions caused during installation, use (energy consumption), repairs, demolition, and disposal of the raw materials.

The life cycle runs from the cradle to the grave. It begins with the extraction of raw material, extends over the use of the product, its recycling, and then finally to its disposal [14]. The life cycle phases of buildings can be divided into manufacture, erection, use, and disposal. Each of these phases has energy and material flows. The flows can be traced back to resources extracted from the environment, the generation of the required energy, the production of the building materials, transport, the erection of buildings, their use, demolition, and disposal (Figures 7 and 8) [15] [17]. It is important to make careful, considerate use of the raw materials and resources in the manufacture of the products.

Environmental impacts cannot be shown for all life cycle phases because the necessary data are not available.

Because the life cycle assessment is also dependent on the applied loading and fire protection requirements, it is calculated using project-specific values related to a square meter of component surface.

Type III environmental product declarations (EPD) offer architects and clients a way of informing themselves about the environmental aspects of building products. They can then compare products and influence resource consumption by their choice of building products during the design phase of a building [16].

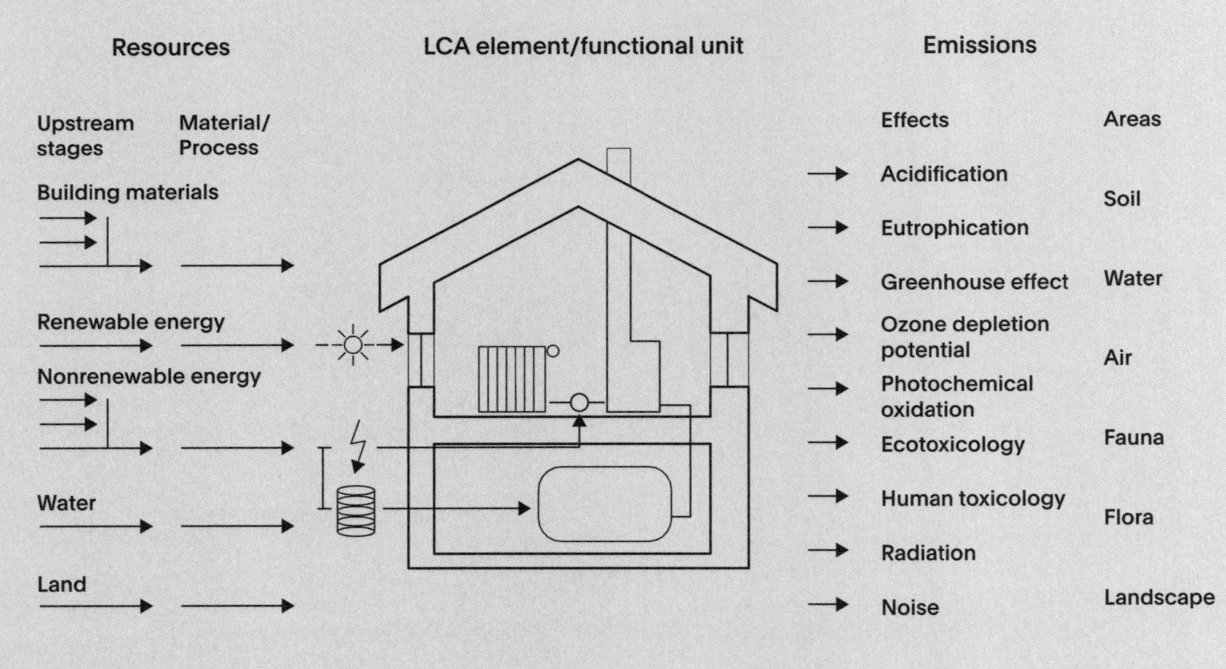

A   18   7
Material and energy flows during the life cycle of a building [13]

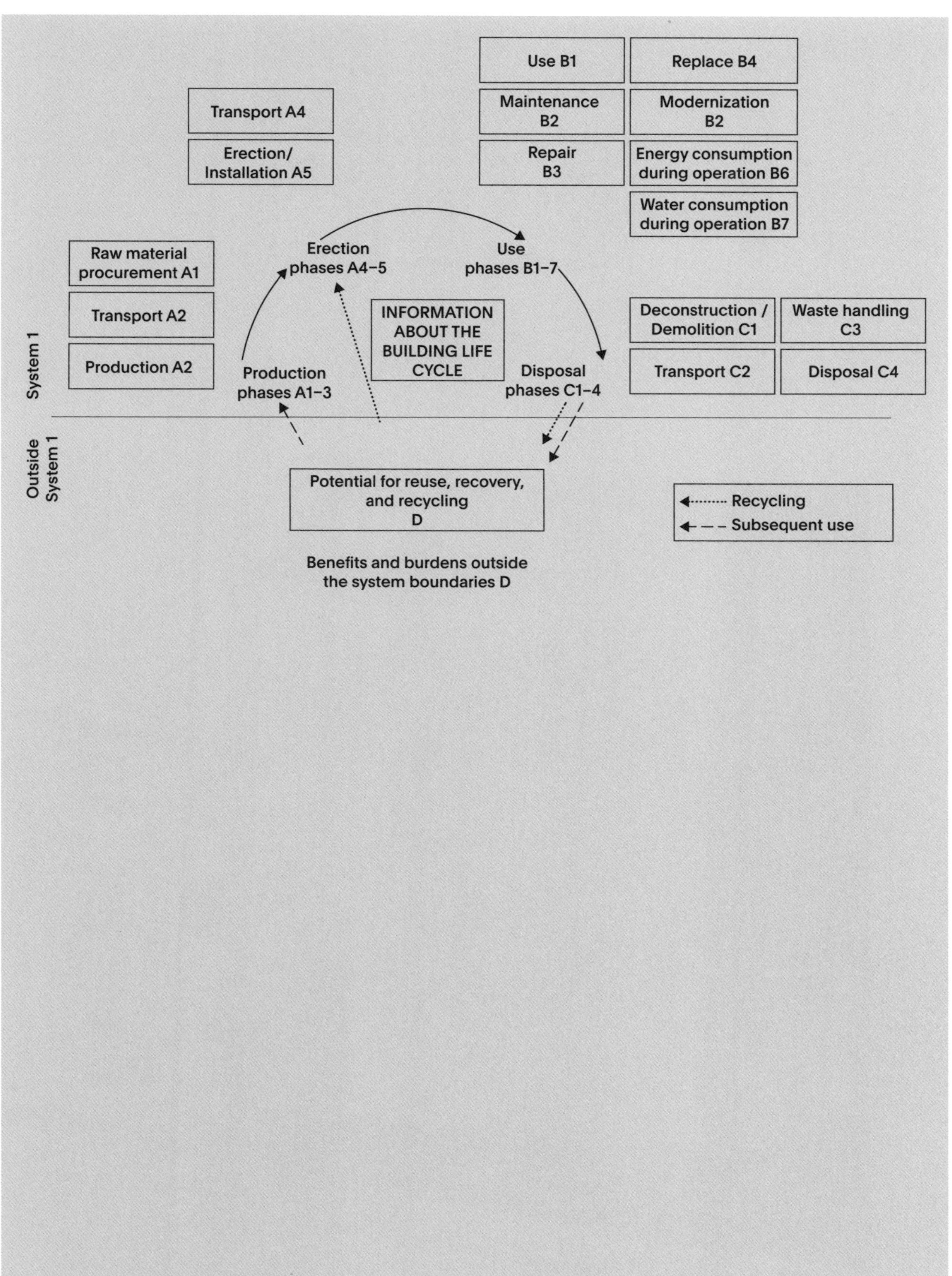

8
Life cycle stages of the building [17],
more detail added

Guide

"Make things as simple as possible, but no simpler."

Albert Einstein

Simple building pursues the goal of protecting the environment throughout the full life cycle of buildings. The result is houses that are simple to build and simple to use. This guide explains which building parameters should be given more attention and why.

The *Building Simply* guide is an attempt to answer the question of the "future of building" with the approach of simplification in the sense of reduction and robustness. The authors are aware that they cannot provide a universally valid building concept. Their intention is much more to stimulate an iterative process in which building gradually becomes simpler, more sustainable, and more efficient—in short, more holistic.

Content and Application

This guide summarizes the principles identified in the research project. It enables stakeholders to gain a deeper insight into the strategy of simple building. The chapters start from the choice of building form and then deal with architectural and engineering design, looking at the building as a whole then diving into the details. They explain which project parameters are particularly important and why. The necessary basic knowledge is summarized in separate info boxes, with references to the source information should the reader wish to know more. At the end of every section is a discussion of how the principle has been implemented in the research houses.

B1   Compactness

"Reduce the area of the building envelope. Increase building density."

Apartment on above-ground floor

Living area 72 m²

Tiny House

Living area 18 m²

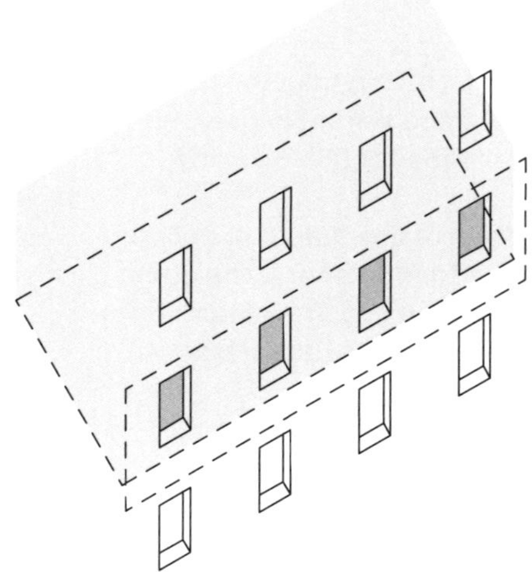

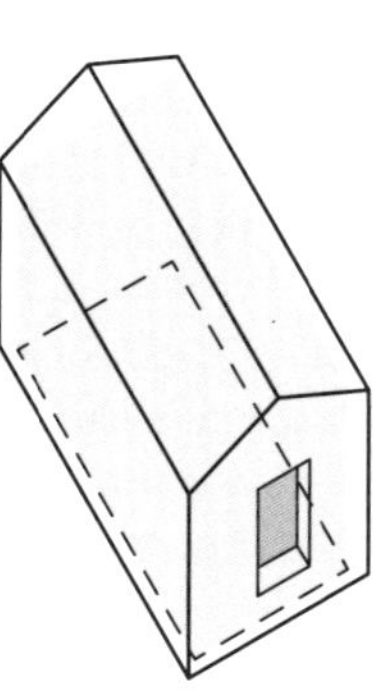

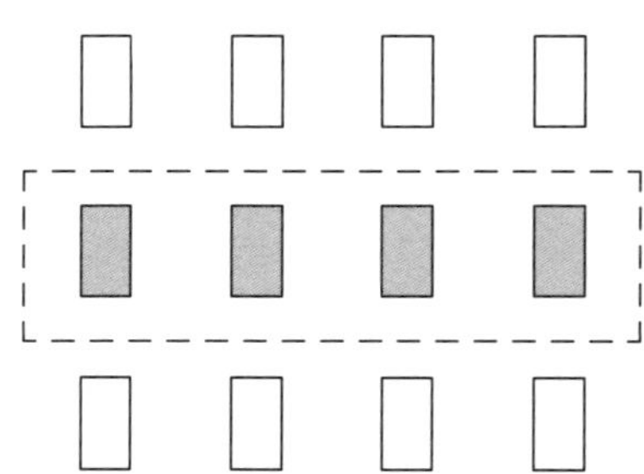

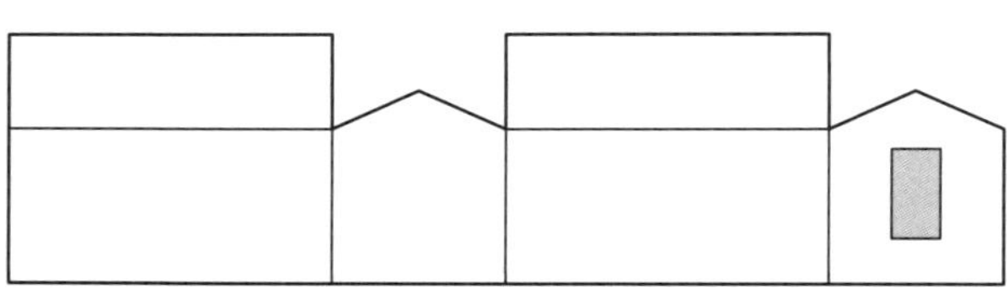

Building envelope in contact with outdoor air

42 m²

Building envelope in contact with outdoor air

89 m²

10
Comparison of a city apartment with
a tiny house in terms of living and
building envelope areas

Compactness

The comparison of a city apartment with a tiny house makes it clear: even when the living area is reduced to 18 m², the building envelope—that is, the roof, external wall, and window—is twice as big as that of a 72 m² apartment on the top floor of a multistory building.

External walls and roofs are the most expensive surface-forming components in a building. In comparison to internal walls and ceilings, their manufacture costs an additional 15–300 EUR/m² [18]. Reducing the building envelope therefore saves money.

Components forming the building envelope are more expensive because they have to be insulated. Insulation obstructs the flow of heat energy from hot to cold. In winter, therefore, an insulated building loses less heat to the environment through its external skin.

Insulating external walls and roofs well makes good sense. However, reducing the area of the external skin itself is even better. There are two strategies to achieve this:

- Reduction of living area
  If the living area is designed efficiently, that is, reduced, then the required building skin is also reduced.
- Compact design
  The areas of the external walls and roof are reduced with respect to the living area. Urban block edge development, for example, naturally lends itself to this approach (see Figure 10).

If both strategies—that is, the reduction in living area and a compact design—are combined, then this directly reduces the amount of material used and the energy consumption during operation. At the same time, environmental impacts such as land use, transport infrastructure provision, and traffic volumes are often also positively affected. It is important to recognize that questions of building density should not be discussed and decided only in the interests of individuals but also at the communal, political, and societal levels. Whether it is possible to use these two strategies singly or combined depends on the wishes of the people involved, the site, and the surroundings.

The research houses in Bad Aibling each offer a living area of 400 m² with a building envelope area of 870 m². The ratio of approximately 1:2 compares favorably with a tiny house (approx. 1:5) and unfavorably with the apartment on the top floor of a block edge development building (approx. 2:1). The development plan for the area had to be changed to allow the research houses to be built in this form on the site.

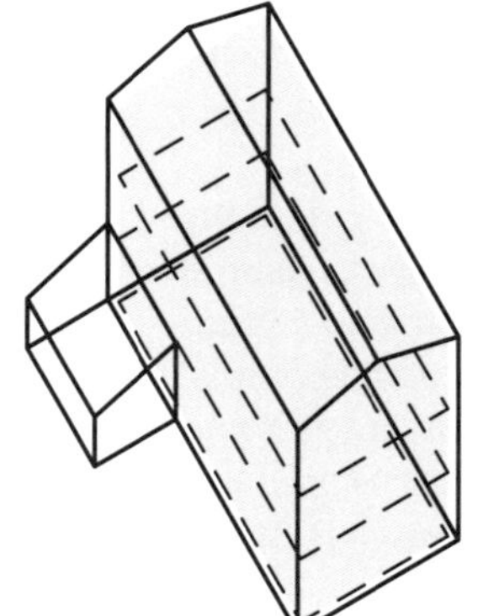

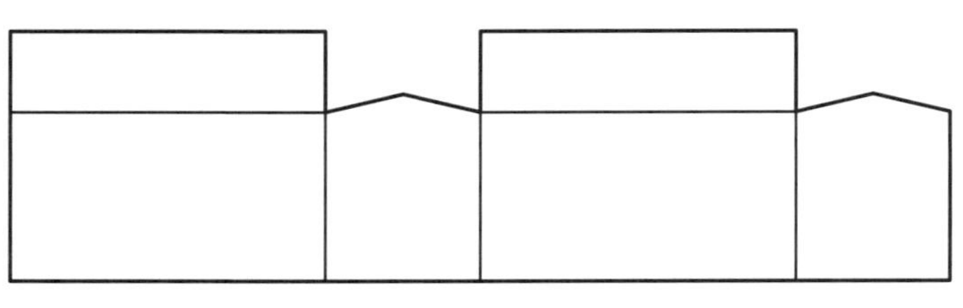

Research house

Living area 400 m²

Building envelope in contact with outdoor air

870 m²

B1   24   11
Living and building envelope area of
a research house in Bad Aibling

Compactness

B2 Windows

"The window glass area should equal 10–15 percent of the room area to be lit.
Dispense with the use of solar control glazing."

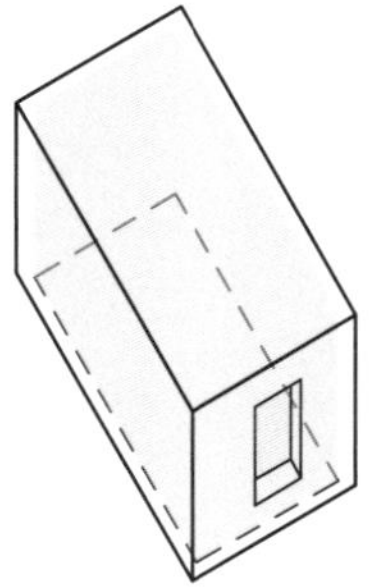
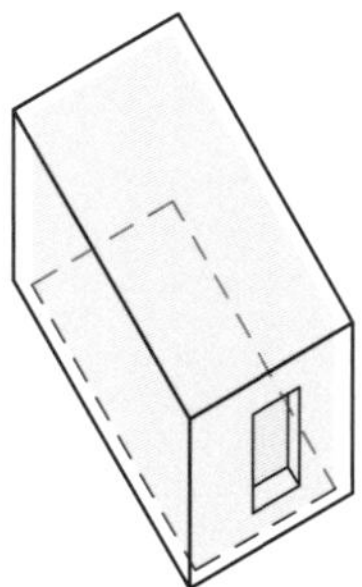
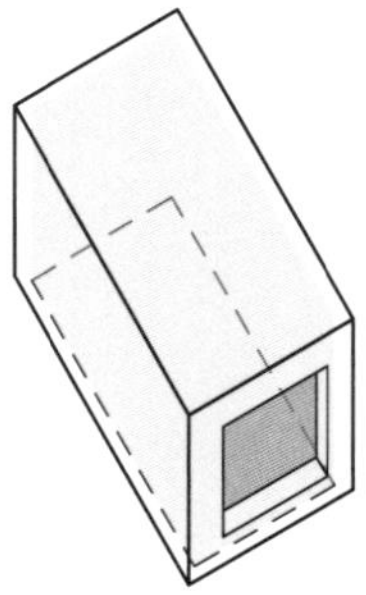
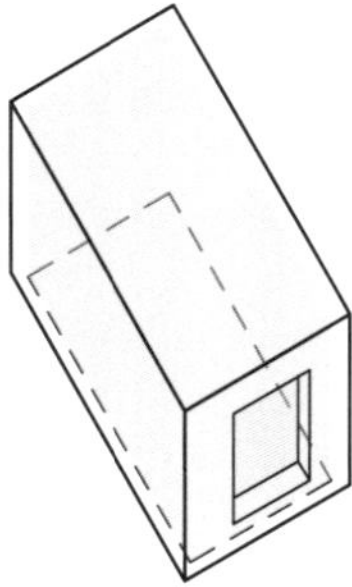
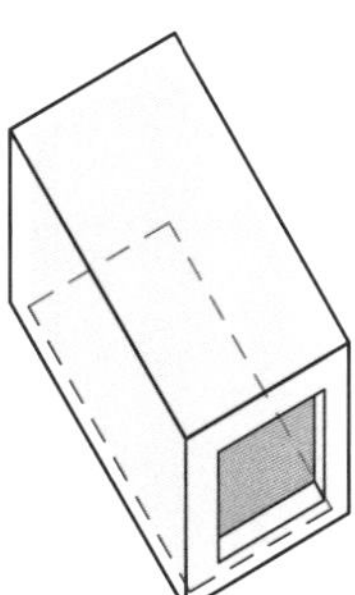

Two glass panes	2-pane insulating glazing	2-pane solar control glazing	3-pane insulating glazing	3-pane solar control glazing
T_{vis} = 82 %	T_{vis} = 81 %	T_{vis} = 37 %	T_{vis} = 71 %	T_{vis} = 36 %
Required glass area 2.01 m²	Required glass area 2.04 m²	Required glass area 4.46 m²	Required glass area 2.32 m²	Required glass area 4.58 m²

The window has an important role to play as the transition between indoor and outdoor space. Every window gives a view to the outside and the option of ventilation. Daylight provision in the room depends mainly on three factors: window size, type of glass, and where it is installed.

The size and type of glass are directly related. Typical types of glass are compared in the figure above. The first example shows two separate panes of glass placed one behind the other, which was the practice in earlier times and is still common today. This is followed by four of the most commonly used types of insulating glazing. These panes are fixed to one another at their edges and the cavity between them is filled with special gases to increase the insulating effect of the glazing. The solar control glazing has a coating that reflects a proportion of solar radiation.

12
How large does the window have to be to supply the room with the same amount of light for different types of glass?

How much light enters the room therefore depends on the quality of the window glass: 3-pane insulating glazing lets through 71 percent of visible light. In the case of 3-pane solar control glazing, this is only 36 percent; the remaining part is reflected by the applied coating.

The area of the glazing must be selected, depending on the type of glass, to ensure the room receives sufficient daylight. With solar control glass, the glazing must therefore be twice as large to admit the same amount of light into the room.

Solar radiation
per day in December
720 WH/m²

Outdoor temperature
0.7 °C

Indoor temperature
22 °C

Compass direction
south

Room dimensions H × W × D
3 × 6 × 3 m

Glass parameters
Light transmittance: T_{vis}
Total solar energy
transmittance: g
Thermal transmittance: U_g

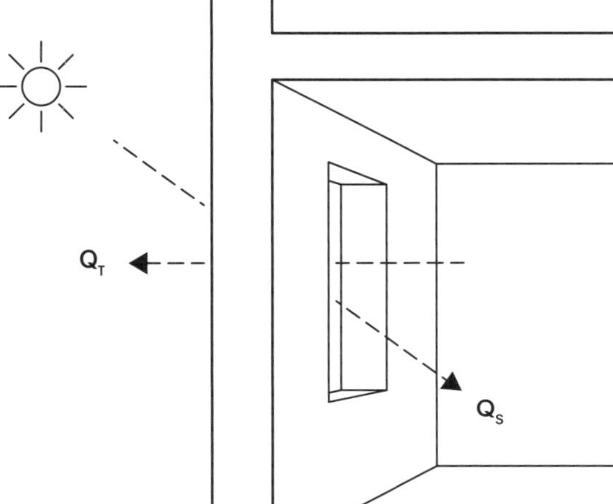

	T_{vis} (Light)	Required area of glass	g (Energy)	Q_s Solar gain	U_g W/m²*K (Heat)	Q_T Heat loss	Energy balance 24 h
Two glass panes	82 %	2.01 m²	77 %	1115 Wh	2.95	-3034 Wh	-1919 Wh
2-pane insulating glazing	81 %	2.04 m²	74 %	1085 Wh	1.18	-1229 Wh	-144 Wh
2-pane solar control glazing	37 %	4.46 m²	23 %	738 Wh	1.12	-2553 Wh	-1815 Wh
3-pane insulating glazing	71 %	2.32 m²	49 %	820 Wh	0.63	-748 Wh	72 Wh
3-pane solar control glazing	36 %	4.58 m²	20 %	660 Wh	0.62	-1452 Wh	-792 Wh

27   13
Energy assessment of south-facing glazing: what effect do different glass types have on the room's energy balance?

The choice of glass also has implications for the energy balance. Energy moves through windows in two different ways. First, the daylight and thermal radiation from the sun enters the room as heat energy. This is called solar gain (Qs). Second, heat can move in two directions through the window when the indoor and outdoor temperatures differ. This is described as transmission heat loss (Qt). This effect is particularly large in winter. Both effects take place at the same time.

The above comparison shows the overall balance for a day-night cycle. The columns give the total energy gains and losses over this period. It is assumed that the window faces south, the room temperature is 22 °C and the outdoor temperature is 0.7 °C. The value for solar radiation is derived empirically for the month of December [19].

The glazing consisting of two panes arranged one behind the other has a negative energy balance. The heat losses (3,034 Wh) are greater than the solar gains (1,115 Wh). Therefore, 1,919 Wh must be supplied to the room, otherwise the indoor temperature will drop. This is approximately the amount of energy a 2,000 W microwave consumes in an hour of continuous operation.

The insulating glazing has a better energy balance. The 2-pane version requires 144 Wh, while the 3-pane insulating glazing achieves plus 72 Wh, an overall energy gain.

The result for the solar control glazing is surprisingly poor. The 3-pane solar control glazing produces a loss of 792 Wh. The 2-pane version produces a loss of 1,815 Wh, almost as poor a performance as the traditional two separate panes found in old buildings.

One of the reasons for this is that the solar control glazing is more than twice as large in order to admit sufficient daylight and is therefore also responsible for more heat loss. The greater part of the poor performance, however, was due to the solar control coating, which reduces solar gain.

Therefore 2- or 3-pane insulation glazing should be used without a solar control coating. The size of the window should be selected such that adequate daylight enters the room. As a rule of thumb, the size of the glazed area should be approximately 10–15 percent of the area of the room to ensure that it is adequately lit and neither solar control glazing nor solar screening is necessary.

The compass direction plays no significant role in the provision of daylight to the room. On cloudy days, when daylight provision would be most critical, the defused proportion of sunlight is almost 100 percent. Therefore, compass direction has no effect in this case [20].

The installation situation is important. Under an overcast sky, the light from the zenith is about three times stronger than the light from the horizon. High rooms with high-set windows bring a lot of daylight into the room from an area close to the zenith. Light from two or more sides creates equal brightness with balanced contrasts [21].

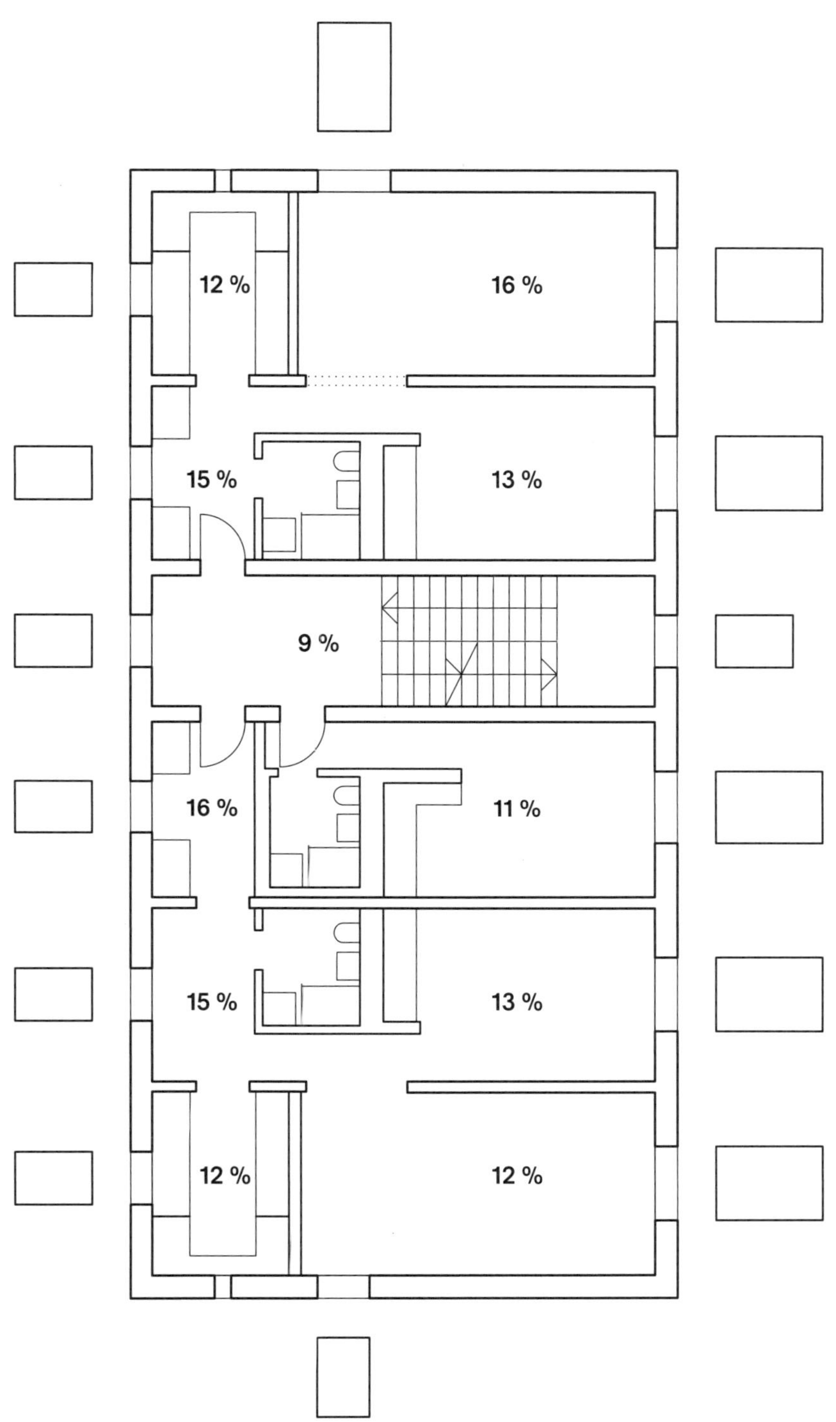

29 14
First floor of a research house:
Ratio of the glazed surface area of the
window to the room area to be lit

Implementation in the Research Houses

3-pane insulating glazing was used for the research houses. The triple-glazed units admitted 70 percent of the visible part of solar radiation. In this case, the ratio of the glazed area to the room area was between 12 and 16 percent in the apartment rooms and 9 percent in the stairwell. The amount of solar heat entering through the windows in summer is not very high because the windows are no larger than necessary to provide a reasonable level of daylight. The windows are set on the internal face of the wall. The reveals cast a shadow onto the windows and thus reduce the amount of heat admitted.

15
Full-scale models of the windows and surrounding components were built to verify the detail of the installation and window function

Windows

B3   Thermal Inertia

"Heavy construction stores the heat.
Night ventilation cools the thermal mass."

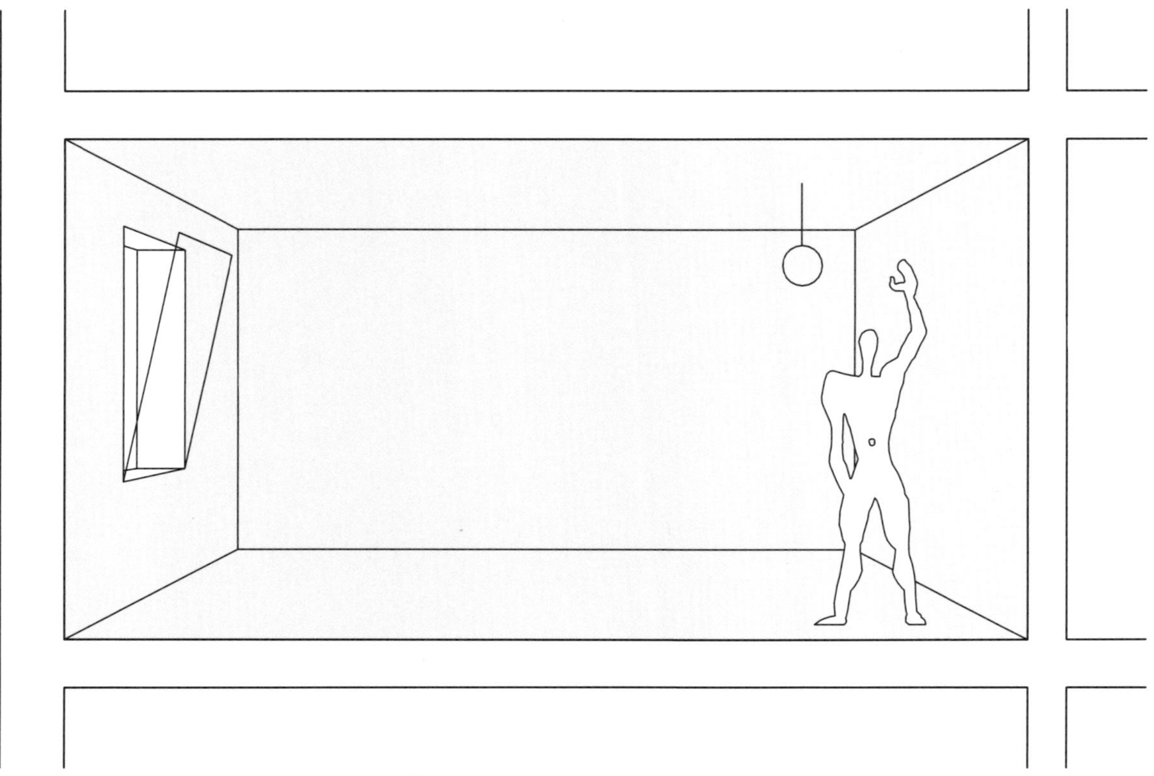

Heat up room components
by 1 degree:
2,500–5,500Wh

Buildings with a high mass exhibit thermal inertia. Everyone knows that places such as churches or basements also remain cool in summer.

On the other hand, air is the precise opposite of an inert component. It takes very little energy, 18 Wh in fact, to raise the temperature of the air in a room with a volume of 55 m^3 by one degree. That is the equivalent of the heat that two people give off in five minutes or that enters a room through a normal south-facing window in five minutes from the midday sun [22].

B3   32   16
Energy required to warm the room air
or the room-enclosing components

Were it not for the thermal inertia of the building, it would soon become very warm inside the room. The building can be thought of as a thermal "battery" that can continually compensate for the temperature of the indoor air. The capacity of this battery depends on the type of construction of the building. In the case of lightweight building construction, the capacity of each room is 2,500 Wh/K, whereas with heavyweight construction the capacity is 5,500 Wh/K. This means that 2.5–5.5 kWh of heat energy is required in order to raise the temperature of all the components enclosing the room by one degree. We observed the way the battery works on a summer's day: whenever the temperature in the room rises by one degree, the ceiling and walls cool it down again. There needs to be 140 to 300 of these cycles before the temperature of the ceiling and walls rises by one degree. The battery continues to function even though the whole system is now one degree warmer. In the night that follows, the energy flow reverses. When cooler air enters the room, the ceiling and walls cool down again. The battery is then recharged for the next summer's day.

This comparison with a battery helps in considering how large the thermal inertia of the building needs to be in practice. A small battery is enough if it is not too highly loaded and is regularly charged. If the room is sheltered from the sun and night cooling takes place on a regular cycle, then lightweight construction is adequate. If the room receives a lot of sun or the design envisages no nighttime cooling over several consecutive nights, then it is worthwhile having a large battery, that is, for the building to have a lot of components with thermal inertia. Furnishings and furniture can slow down the effects of thermal inertia, because these items cover surfaces and reduce the exchange of energy between the room air and the walls and floor. Therefore, in an occupied building the ceiling has the greatest influence.

If the room air warms up particularly quickly, there is a further effect. The temperature we perceive is actually not only dependent on the ambient air but also on the temperature of the surfaces surrounding us. This means that as long as the temperature of the surrounding surfaces such as walls and ceilings remains constant, we perceive the warming of the room air as less uncomfortable. The technical term for this is operative temperature. This is calculated as the mean of the air temperature and radiation temperature of the surrounding surfaces.

Five-minute purge ventilation in winter of a room with a lot of thermal inertia works very well. A short time after the window has been closed again, we find the room pleasantly warm although the whole of the stale room air has been replaced by cooler outdoor air. The operative temperature will fall only slightly; the components will always quickly warm the room air up again.

Implementation in the Research Houses

All three research houses have a reinforced concrete ceiling. The structural internal walls are constructed in concrete, solid wood, or solid blocks, depending on the type of construction. These walls have a high degree of thermal inertia, and the system is robust. The concrete building has the greatest storage mass at 5,600 Wh/K per room, which is around 300 times that of the enclosed air. The timber building at 3,300 Wh/K per room also falls into the category of heavyweight construction. The masonry building at 4,400 Wh/K per room falls almost exactly between the other two.

17
**Use of a pivoting window promotes
effective window ventilation**

A further link in the chain for using the thermal inertia of building components is the ability to effectively ventilate during cool summer nights. The key to this in almost all residential buildings is to have several windows on different sides to allow cross ventilation. This works particularly well because even a light wind will ensure good ventilation in the apartment. Another way of enabling effective night ventilation is to use pivoting windows (see Figure 17). This type of window pivots from the middle. Even when only slightly open, a good amount of air flows in and out of the room, because there is an opening at the top and the bottom. Warm air exits through the top and cold air enters through the bottom.

For a typical week in August, we measured the indoor climate in an east-facing one-room apartment. The results are displayed in Figure 18. The three lines represent the outdoor temperature, the room temperature, and the radiation temperature respectively. The outdoor temperature was between almost 30 °C on Wednesday afternoon and approximately 6 °C during Friday night. It should be noted that the room temperature always increases in the morning, when the sun is positioned directly to the east. The radiation temperature (that is, the mean temperature of all surfaces in the room) remains almost constant. The measurements show very well how the thermal inertia of the components has a compensating effect on the indoor climate.

In preparation for the long-term measurements in the research houses, we performed computer simulations of the indoor climate for all three buildings. The room temperatures in all three forms of construction remained in the comfortable range throughout the simulated year. We wait in anticipation to see whether the results match what happens in reality.

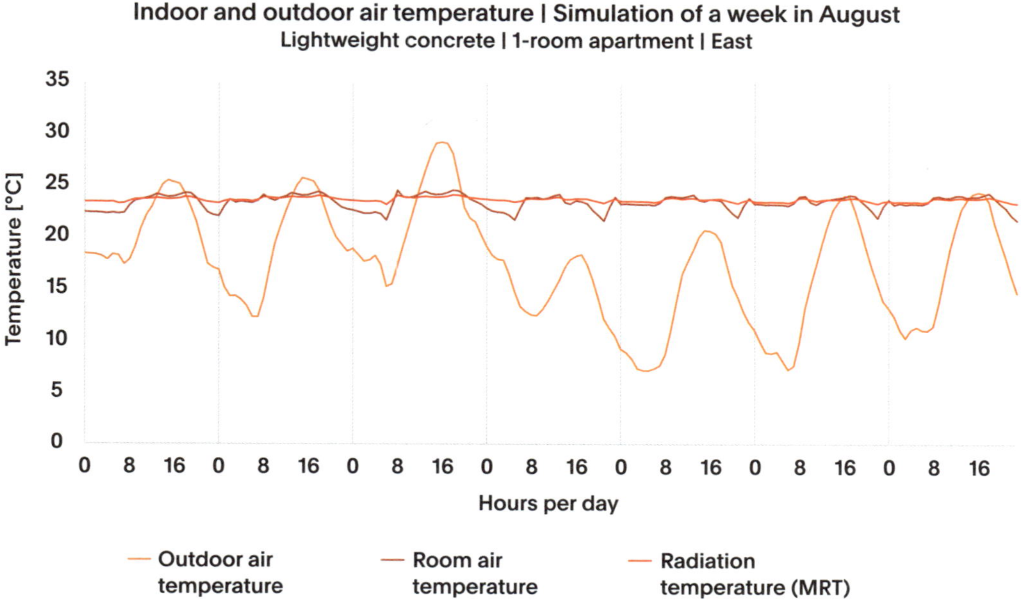

18
The simulation results for a week in August show that the temperatures remain pleasantly constant

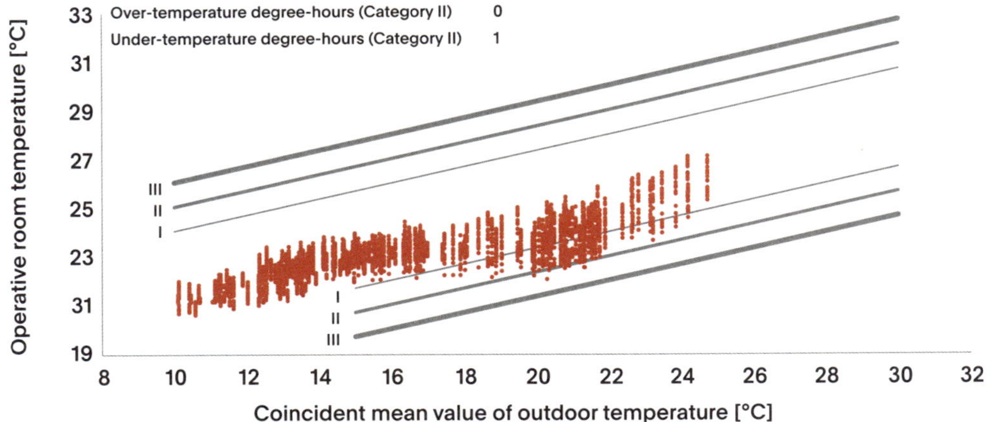

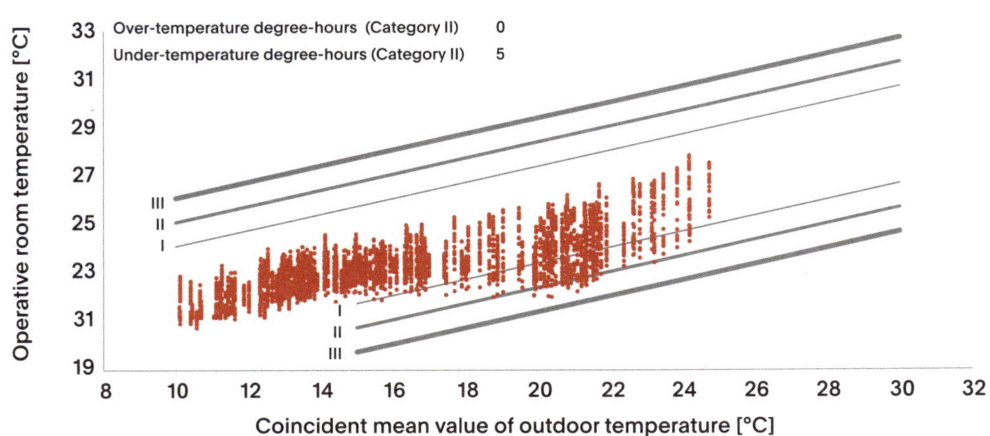

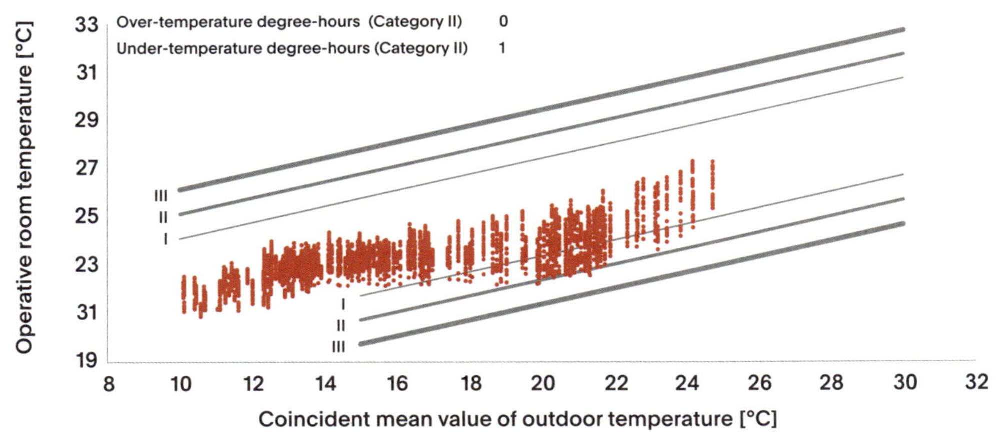

B3   36   19
The simulation showed that for all
three forms of construction, the indoor
climate was comfortable in summer

Thermal Inertia

B4 Robust Technical Systems

"Use robust and reduced technical systems.
Take into account the behavior of the users."

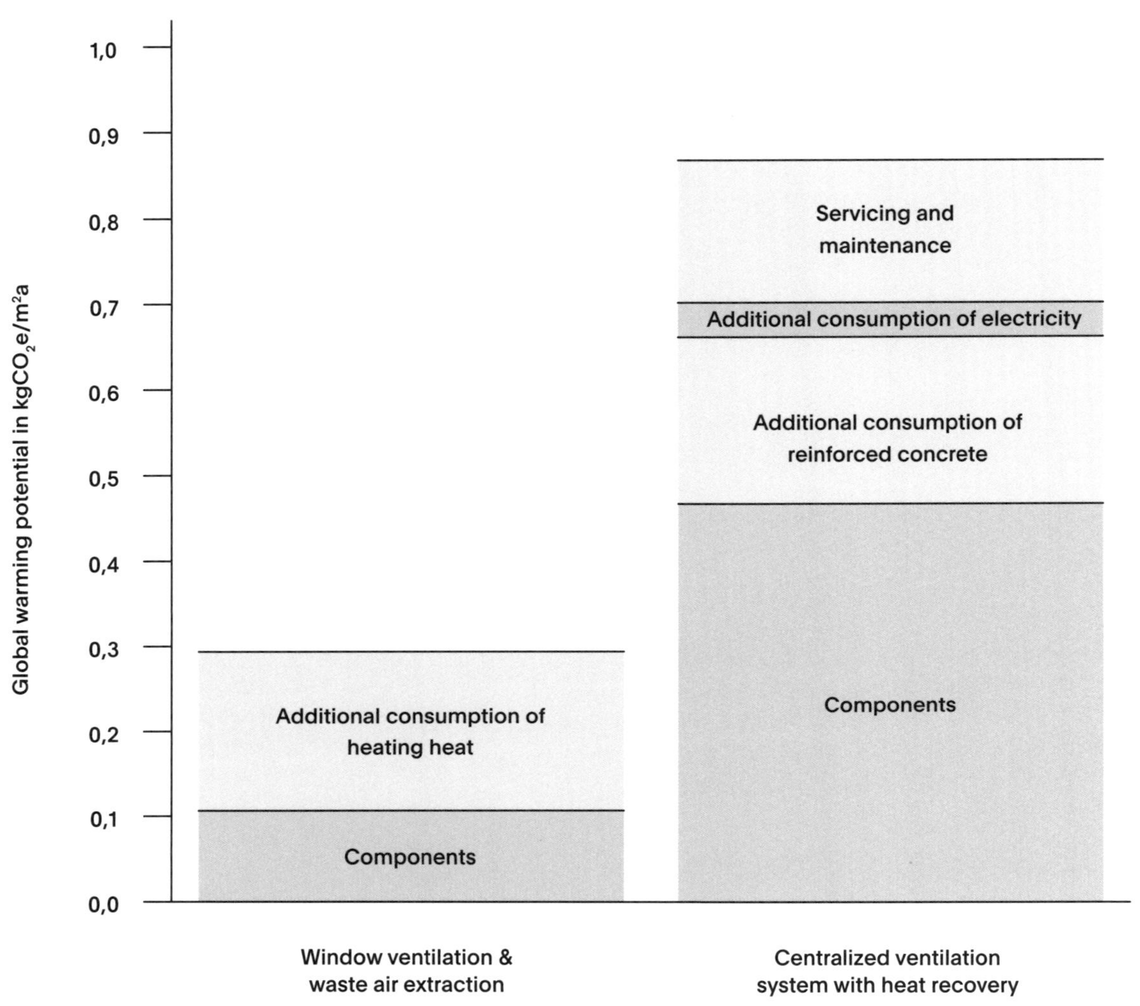

20
The environmental impact of different ventilation systems of the Klee residential development in Zürich-Affoltern related to 1 m² of heated usable area and one year; own chart following [23]

About 20 percent of the whole life cycle cost of the building is incurred during the planning and construction phase. The remaining 80 percent of the cost occurs in the use phase.

The major part of this cost is energy consumption. Attempts to reduce this consumption have continued over the years, for example by installing or retrofitting insulation. Technical systems, for example air-conditioning with heat recovery, are popularly believed to reduce a building's energy consumption, the associated costs, and negative environmental impact.

However, the example in Figure 20 shows that these measures frequently do not achieve the desired savings: The researchers took long-term measurements of the data from ventilation systems for the Klee residential development in Zürich-Affoltern [23]. Centralized ventilation systems with heat recovery containing a large number of components were compared over the whole life cycle with the simple concept of window ventilation and bathroom extractor fans. The findings of the comparison concluded that the additional expenditure on technical equipment, operating energy, maintenance, and servicing far exceeded the anticipated savings in heat energy. Figure 20 also shows that the centralized ventilation system has triple the negative impact on global warming (greenhouse gas potential) compared with the window ventilation and bathroom extractor fan option.

When the theoretically calculated values differ from the results measured in practice, this is often called the performance gap [24]. The performance gap between design and operation occurs mainly at the level of building services and user behavior [24] [25]. The concept of simple building seeks to keep this gap as small as possible by adopting reduced and robust technical concepts.

First we would like to briefly describe three of the most important effects this gap creates, which have been investigated many times [24] [25] [26].

1. User behavior is wrongly assumed.

Users do not behave in the way designers predict: in energy-optimized buildings, higher average indoor temperatures and more frequent opening of windows are observed during the heating season. This means that the way users behave causes them to waste more energy than estimated in buildings with higher living comfort. This effect is called the rebound effect [27].

In contrast to this, users in old buildings behave in a more energy-saving way than predicted. For example, in the latter case only part of the apartment or building is heated or only reduced ventilation takes place. This is known as the prebound effect [27].

Another reason is the static comfort models and simplified calculation method given in the standard, which do not depict users realistically or flexibly enough [28] [29] [30]. There have been several studies involving the collection of behavioral data since the 1950s [31]. Up to now the theory has been based on statistical models, which in turn have used these empirical data sets [32]. However, these data have been collected from a limited number of users, whose sensitivity to comfort was tested only in the laboratory.

2. Technical systems do not work properly.

Whoever operates technical systems or designs in the building energy field may often find that, for example, the settings for the underfloor heating are not switched from "manual" to "automatic" on installation, or the photovoltaic system feeds no PV electricity into the public grid for the lack of an understandable system description [33]. Without regular and consistent checks—and for that matter without monitoring—people remain unaware of these faults, although they are easy to rectify and have a large influence on energy consumption.

Other behaviors observed particularly in multistory residential construction include: despite their buildings having mechanical ventilation and heat recovery, users open windows, with the result that the actual energy demand is many times the calculated value. With naturally ventilated buildings, on the other hand, the actual energy demand equates to or is even slightly below the calculated value. Mechanical ventilation in multistory residential buildings does not represent a robust solution [35].

3. The power consumed in operating technical systems is underestimated.

In general, high-quality, low-power consumption components for technical building services equipment are available on the market today. However, the art, like completing a jigsaw, lies in putting these components together in such a way that the system functions properly and the constituent parts work in coordination with one another. This is made clear, for example, with energy-efficient pumps: despite energy-saving technology, the pressure losses in hydraulic systems are far too high, which means the pump's energy demand is also often unnecessarily high. Poorly set operating points and incorrect design lead to these high energy values.

To reduce the above effects and close the performance gap, the design of the technical systems should seek to achieve the following goals:

1. Users do the regulating themselves.

Instead of complex control systems that regulate indoor comfort based on static parameters, users should adaptively control their systems according to what their senses tell them (user interaction). It is also worthwhile raising the importance of this approach with users so that they can avoid wasting energy where possible (user awareness). Experience shows that people feel thermally more comfortable if they can personally intervene in the system [25] [34].

2. As simple as possible!

Install only what is most necessary! Compared to complex systems, simple building technical services systems are less susceptible to system errors, operating errors, and the failure of technical components. Simple technical equipment is also easy to service and modify over the years. Only when a technical system can be understood in its

Robust Technical Systems

entirety can the original designers and the later modifiers make correct decisions. Simple building services—that is, robust, passive, and at the same time user-regulated—lead not only to a reduced energy demand and lower installation costs, they also raise user satisfaction (see Point 1. Users do the regulating themselves) and reduce the performance gap.

3. Correctly assess technical equipment.

The less the technical equipment in a building is required to operate, the less energy is required to operate the building. Additional technical equipment should be used only if this can function correctly if the actual behavior of the users deviates from the assumed. The assessment should include not only the cost of the additional technical equipment but also the space it requires, the servicing cost, and energy consumption in operation —and the future environmental impact in the form of its greenhouse gas potential

Implementation in the Research Houses

In the research houses, users control the fresh air inflow through the windows. Heat is supplied on-site from an existing biogas combined heat and power plant. Heating is controlled by thermostatic valves on the radiators; lighting by light switches.

The simple actions of ordinary living, such as breathing, cooking, showering, drying, washing, or keeping indoor plants, produce additional moisture in the room. This moisture can damage the building if it is not removed often enough by ventilating. For example, the moisture in the air can condense on the internal face of an external wall. The moistened components can provide a site for fungus or mold to grow. With the aim of preventing this situation, some house rental agreements stipulate the minimum amount of ventilation that tenants have to ensure takes place. The objective of these clauses is to control moisture in the air. The problem with this is that responsibility for moisture damage is transferred to the tenants.

The research houses were designed to allow the residents to behave as they like. There is no compulsory ventilation requirement. With the windows closed, the minimum level of air changes to provide protection against moisture is achieved through ventilation slots in the window frame, often called window rebate vents. The air changes are induced by the exhaust air fans in the internal bathrooms. These are fitted with a moisture sensor to allow a 3 W fan to suck air out of the room until the threshold of 60 percent relative humidity is reached. If the bath is used, the exhaust air fan operates at its normal high setting (6 W). Switching the light on gives the signal to the fan to operate normally.

The long-term monitoring system collects data on the energy consumption, indoor climate, and users' behavior over a period of two years. The collected data can be analyzed to show how the strategy employed in the research houses worked in practice. The data also allows a better understanding of user behavior. This will help ensure future optimizations are compatible with what happens in practice. The collected data can also be analyzed to audit the previously used simulation tools and calibrate them for the future.

Heating device

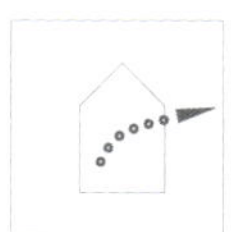
Exhaust air extracted via wet cell

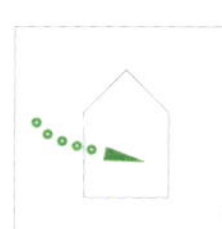
Natural window ventilation on one side + night ventilation opening in window frames

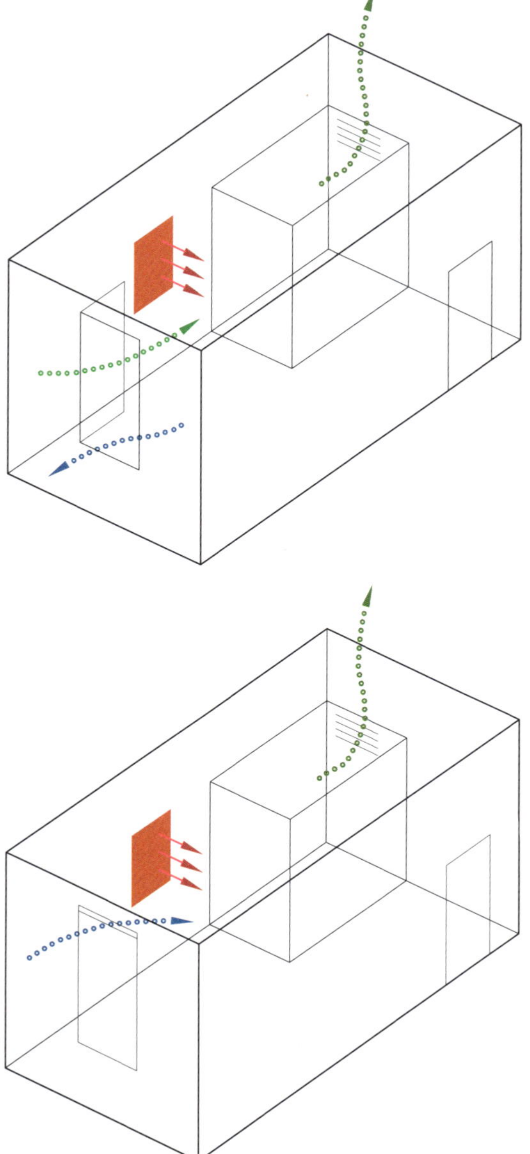

Robust Technical Systems

21
Research houses in Bad Aibling, schematic diagram of the simple ventilation concept, window ventilation with bathroom fan; graphic produced by TUM

"Consider future uses. Design for variants.
Separate the technical systems from the building construction."

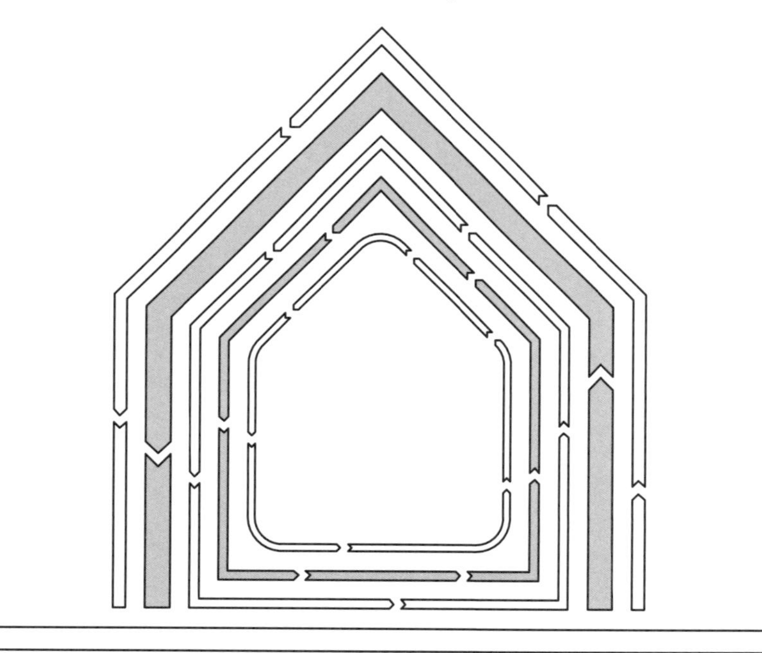

People think of buildings as being static. In German, for example, the word for real estate is "Immobilie", which suggests immobility. In contrast, the same language's word for furnishings, "Mobiliar", suggests mobility. However, when a building is considered over a time span of 100 years or longer, it soon becomes clear: many parts of the building go through several cycles of change. What the service lives of various parts of the house depend on and how they can be extended is explained in the info box "Service Life of Building Components."

B5   44   22
                                           Service life of component layers in
                                           accordance with [35]

Service Life of Building Components

An accurate assessment of the anticipated service life of a building and its parts is essential for an economically and ecologically sustainable design and prevents casual, superficial economic decisions in the planning and construction phase [36].

The estimated service life of building components and materials is determined by various factors. First there is the quality of the component; this includes not just the manufacture and storage but also the transport and material quality. Building designers are responsible for the construction quality—for example, how components are protected by specific features of the building, such as by canopies, construction details that protect wood, and sacrificial timber cladding. The quality of construction depends on the people employed on-site, but is also affected by climatic conditions. Designers should take into account the anticipated conditions of use, with particular reference to the intensity of use and the likely quality of maintenance [36]. The theoretical consideration of the rate of deterioration of a component (see Figure 23) shows that repairs and technical improvements can raise the quality of these components to make them even better than they were when first installed (for example, by sanding and oiling floorboards or replacing fittings and seals around the windows).

By taking into account the influence factors indicated above, long-term functionality is likely to be achieved and lead to a long technical service life. In addition to the material-related influence factors, user-specific expectations play an important role in the design of the probable service life.

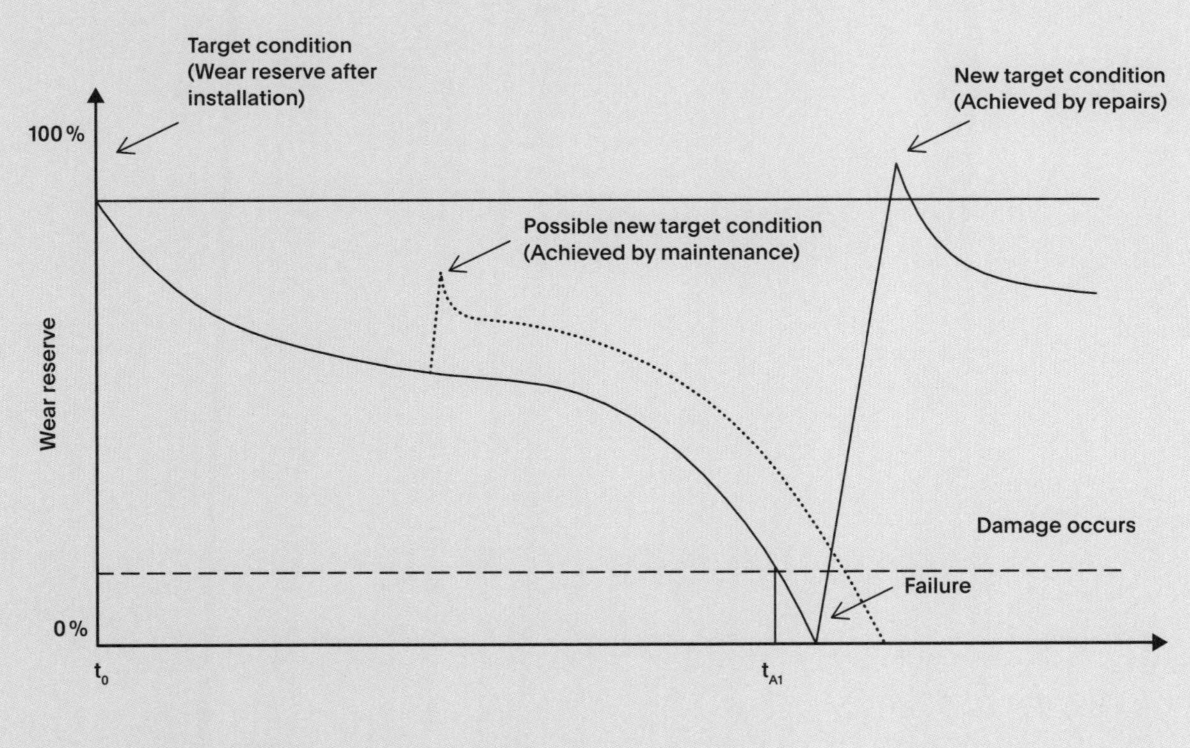

45   23
Theoretical sequence of component wear [36]

Dynamic and individual building histories, different users, and changing aesthetic tastes often lead to redesigns or conversions, even though the components have not yet reached their technical end of life. Ideally, buildings and their components should be designed such that the period of use equates to the whole technical service life.

However, it may be beneficial to take a more nuanced consideration of building components:

- The layout of the building should be made as neutral as possible with regard to its use, so that it allows scope for a wide range of spatial adaptations and modifications.

- Various usage scenarios should be considered at the preliminary design stage.

- This future adaptation can be enabled by using ecologically sustainable and inexpensive materials for the space-enclosing components.

System Separation

Extending the maintenance or replacement cycles as much as possible is a good idea because it delays their eventual reconstruction. Despite these efforts, the time comes when particular components must be replaced or at least modified. A consistent and well-thought-out separation of the various systems in the early design stage makes this future replacement or modification much easier.

Separation here refers specifically to the separation of technical and structural systems. A heating radiator is, for example, much easier to replace than underfloor heating.

Implementation in the Research Houses

The components are manufactured and jointed such that full-area surface-to-surface connections are avoided if possible and all layers of components are accessible and removable or are connected by individual fastenings. This approach makes the parts easier to repair or replace and therefore increases the service life of the whole component.

The designer should also ensure that trades follow one another on-site instead of working at the same time, as is often the case. Overlapping layers should be avoided wherever possible. This not only avoids problems in the sequence of construction but also has the valuable secondary effect that subsequent modifications can take place generally in the reverse order of construction, without causing unnecessary disturbance to the surrounding materials.

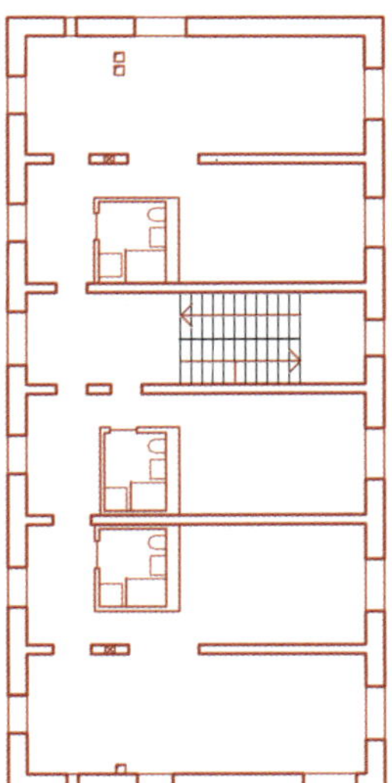
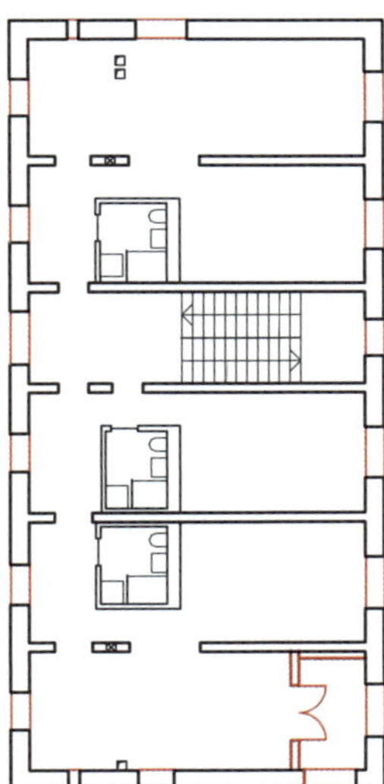
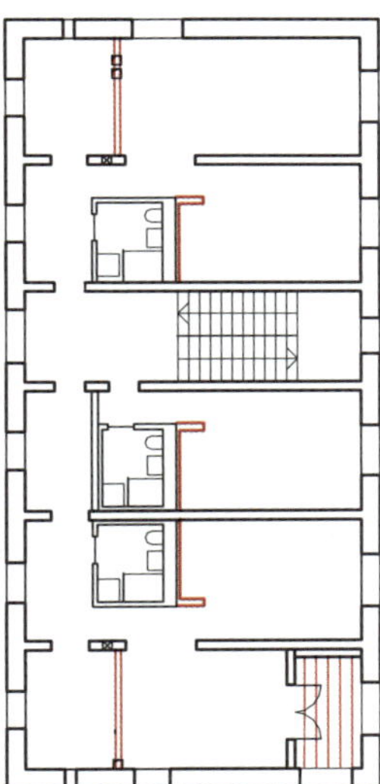
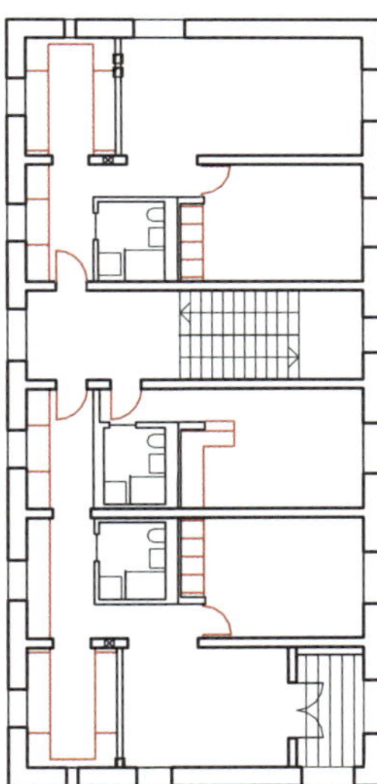

47   24
Construction stages:
shell; envelope; fit-out; fitments

The contractor responsible for constructing the shell does not need to know that a loggia (shown in Figure 24 at the bottom right in plan) is incorporated later. It is not until the fit-out trades install railings instead of windows at the desired location that the facade is set back as a timber frame wall. One effect of this simplification of the construction is that there is a step up on entry to the loggia because insulation for the apartment below is placed there. The example adeptly illustrates the design principle, which is to treat the preceding trade as an existing building. This compels the designer to select a form of construction that makes any adaptations simple to carry out on an existing building many years later. Staying on the example of the loggia: this can be relocated elsewhere in the building at any time.

Separation is also the objective with building services systems. Cabling is bundled in a few riser shafts and led directly to prefabricated bathroom cells through the apartments. All operating elements, such as subdistribution boards and main cut-off switches, are positioned as close as possible to these riser shafts. Cabling from the subdistribution boards is done in skirting board strips or simply installed as surface-mounted equipment.

Main riser shaft visible from two sides

49
26
Loggia, independent of the building
shell

"Layers should be few in number and consist of a single material.
Combine them to form robust and durable constructions."

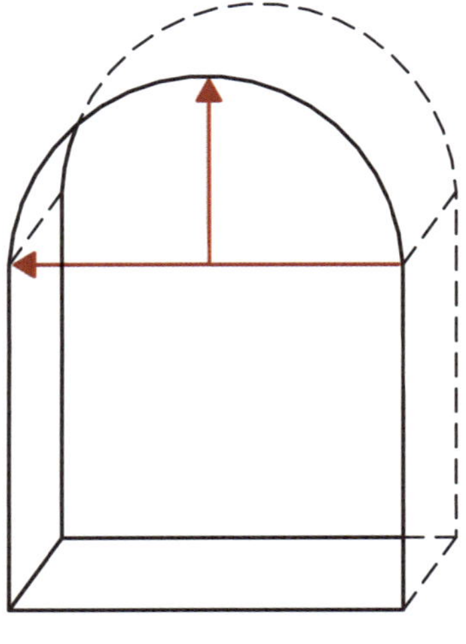

Concrete = circular arch

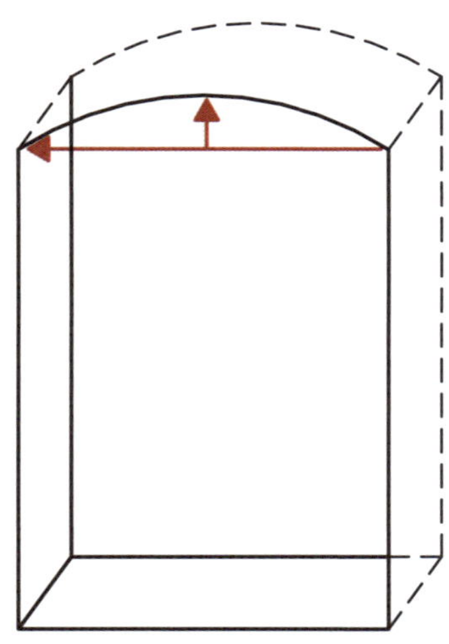

Masonry = segmental arch

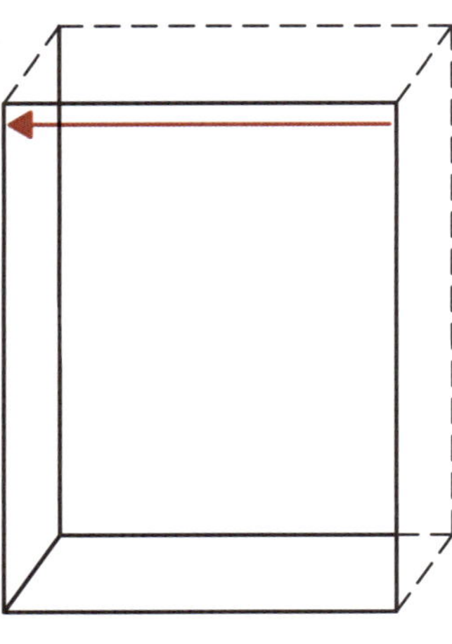

Wood = lintel

Noise, rain, wind, cold, and heat: The external walls protect us from unpleasant environmental influences. At the same time, the external walls are usually part of the load-
bearing structure and are responsible as a facade for the appearance of the house in the
townscape. The requirements placed on external walls have increased in recent years,
particularly with regard to insulation properties. Therefore, external walls are frequently
constructed from several layers, each of which plays a different role.

In normal circumstances, a layer of masonry, reinforced concrete, or timber forms the
load-bearing structure and contributes with its mass to sound insulation and thermal
inertia. The customary layer of insulation usually applied to the outside of the structure
provides the thermal insulation of the external wall. The facade terminates the building as
a design element and weather-screening layer. This strategy is called material layering.

Another strategy is based on material mixtures. Builders' merchants offer all kinds of masonry blocks with an insulating filling. These can be used with special components such as insulated window lintels or special masonry components, for example for use along the support for the ceiling.

The current practice is often to combine both strategies. Looking at the building in the future, the following questions come to mind: When one or more of the layers reaches the end of its service life, how will it be replaced or repaired? Will replacement components for the building continue to be available in the future? Can I reuse the building components elsewhere or separate the mixtures of materials? The basic question is: How sustainable is this building?

The principles to be followed under the slogan "Building Simply" are:

- Low number of component layers

- Use of a single type of mineral or renewable raw materials

- Assembly of components into robust and durable constructions, taking into account the properties of the materials

Monolithic Building

Monolithic building refers generally to the use of a single construction material such as concrete, brick, or timber. The term means "formed from a single block of stone" and comes from Greek. Here it describes the combination of various functions, for example structural support and thermal insulation, in one component. Monolithic building differentiates itself from multiple-layer construction because it fulfills some of the functions of the building in a single component.

Infra-lightweight Concrete

Infra-lightweight concrete is a concrete that is less dense than traditional lightweight concrete. It is also known as ultra lightweight concrete, high-performance lightweight-aggregate concrete, lightweight insulating concrete, and generally as low-density concrete. With a density of less than 800 kg/m³, infra-lightweight concrete is only half as heavy as conventional lightweight concrete and about a quarter of the density of normal weight concrete. It is actually less dense than water. Developments in concrete technology over recent years, above all the work done on optimizing aggregates and admixtures, enable the robust and economic use of the material in modern, sustainable residential building construction [37] [38].

28
The three external wall materials used in the project: Solid wood, brick— clay blocks with air voids—and infra-lightweight concrete

Material-Appropriate Design

The very low density calls for the use of particularly voluminous and lightweight aggregates (such as expanded clay, expanded glass, or foamed glass) and additives such as foaming agents. Being low density, infra-lightweight concrete has a low coefficient of thermal conductivity and a much higher heat insulation performance than conventional normal weight concrete. Thermal conductivity values of 0.185 W/m^{2}K are currently achievable in practice. With this level of thermal conductivity, the German Energy Saving Ordinance (EnEV) 2016 can be complied with using monolithic construction without any additional insulating elements. Due to the comparatively low compressive strengths, wall thicknesses of between 50 and 60 cm are necessary to meet structural requirements. To date, infra-lightweight concrete has been used for two- to three-story buildings, for which project-related approval (ZiE) is necessary in Germany because there is currently no national technical approval (abZ) for the material.

In addition to the pleasant indoor climate and the distinctive appearance of most monolithic buildings, infra-lightweight concrete offers further benefits in terms of building physics. Significant risks such as corrosion or mold growth can be excluded where design and construction has complied with good practice, because reinforcement can be either almost completely omitted or be provided by stainless steel, and aggregates are usually resistant to mold. Making materials or surfaces hydrophobic, in combination with roof overhangs, has proven adequate in practice to prevent the penetration of moisture into the construction, which would otherwise adversely affect the low thermal conductivity. With respect to sound insulation, infra-lightweight concrete, with its absorbent, porous structure, interrupts the transmission of airborne sound. Infra-lightweight concrete is noncombustible and therefore achieves the highest fire protection classification, A1. The material does not smolder or give off harmful emissions in a fire.

Solid Wood

This section discusses solid natural wood and in particular the relatively new cross-laminated timber (CLT) product manufactured from boards glued crosswise to one another. In addition to CLT's added ecological value, it also meets the same performance requirements as a monomaterial for urban buildings as the other two construction materials discussed. Its relatively recent market introduction compared to other building products suggests it has a considerable development potential with regard to material savings, hydrothermal properties, and strength.

The material's low thermal conductivity causes room heat to be stored at the surface for a long time. This is why rooms with predominantly wooden surfaces show a tendency to overheat in response to daily heating cycles in summer. Cross-laminated timber meets health and hygiene requirements because the surfaces are airtight and suppress diffusion, which also makes the use of additional plastic films unnecessary. At the same time, the capillary structure and moisture-storing properties of the surfaces enclosing the rooms help buffer high levels of atmospheric moisture.

The special feature of cross-laminated timber is that it consists almost exclusively of solid wood. The proportion of adhesive in the finished product is less than 1 percent.

Cross-laminated timber is used for structural and nonstructural roof, ceiling, and wall components. It can be used as wall, roof, and ceiling panels or vertical or horizontal beams. Solid wood is a "normally flammable" construction material, which forms an insulating charred layer in fire and, due to its slow-burning behavior of 0.7 mm per minute, reduces the cross section in a controlled manner, enabling members to be deliberately oversized precisely enough to allow for the effects of fire. Good airborne sound attenuation is achieved when used in a two-layer external wall construction in conjunction with weather protection cladding. Very good impact sound attenuation results from the combination of screed and impact sound insulation with low dynamic stiffness, heavy, flexible ceiling cladding, and the integrated additional mass.

Solid wood is a renewable raw material with natural mechanical strength properties. Given sustainable forestry management, it is available in adequate supplies regionally and has additional ecological advantages during its growing phase in that it preserves biodiversity, provides space for recreation, takes up the greenhouse gas CO_2, and stores water. The manufacturer issues an EPD for the cross-laminated timber product and the beneficial environmental effects from the long-term storage of CO_2 as biogenic carbon in solid wood.

Masonry

Highly insulating masonry is an established construction product with a long history. A wealth of knowledge is available about its use as a mono-material. The material has to satisfy rising thermal requirements and therefore undergoes continual further development to bring its thermal insulation properties into line with the other requirements of the European Council's Construction Products Regulation (CPR). Masonry's potential for innovation appears to have sharply declined because improvements over recent years have focused on mixtures of materials rather than its use as a mono-material. Fired blocks manufactured out of porous clay or porous concrete blocks made from an aerated sand-lime mixture which is cast then steam-cured, are used to build external walls out of highly insulating masonry units. In the case of masonry units made from lightweight concrete, the aggregates for cement-bound blocks are highly porous, for example, expanded glass granulate or expanded clay.

Masonry blocks made from brick or lightweight or porous concrete are noncombustible and fulfill the requirements of construction material classification A1. These materials prevent fire spreading and do not give rise to toxic smoke. Health protection and hygiene (healthy housing) are guaranteed by their mineral constituents, which are compatible with building biology, non hazardous to health, and free from allergens and pollutant emissions. Capillary action, the ability to store moisture, in combination with permeability, allows the material to store condensation water in the cold winter months and the monolithic external walls to dry out again over the summer. This ability to store moisture and allow it to diffuse in and out, combined with low thermal conductivity, minimizes the risk of mold formation on the surfaces inside the building and offers sustained protection of the health of the occupants. Masonry units have an adequate insulating effect on airborne sound due to their density and porous structure, and so their thickness is generally determined by the thermal insulation requirements. Special masonry units with a higher bulk density are available where internal walls are required to have high sound insulation properties. In the case of ceilings, impact sound insulation in combination with a heavy ceiling construction provides the necessary sound attenuation. Environmental product declarations, which give details of the resources consumed and environmental impacts of products, are available for the various types of masonry unit.

Material-Appropriate Design

Implementation in the Research Houses

The three research houses in Bad Aibling were completed in monolithic construction in timber, masonry, and lightweight concrete.

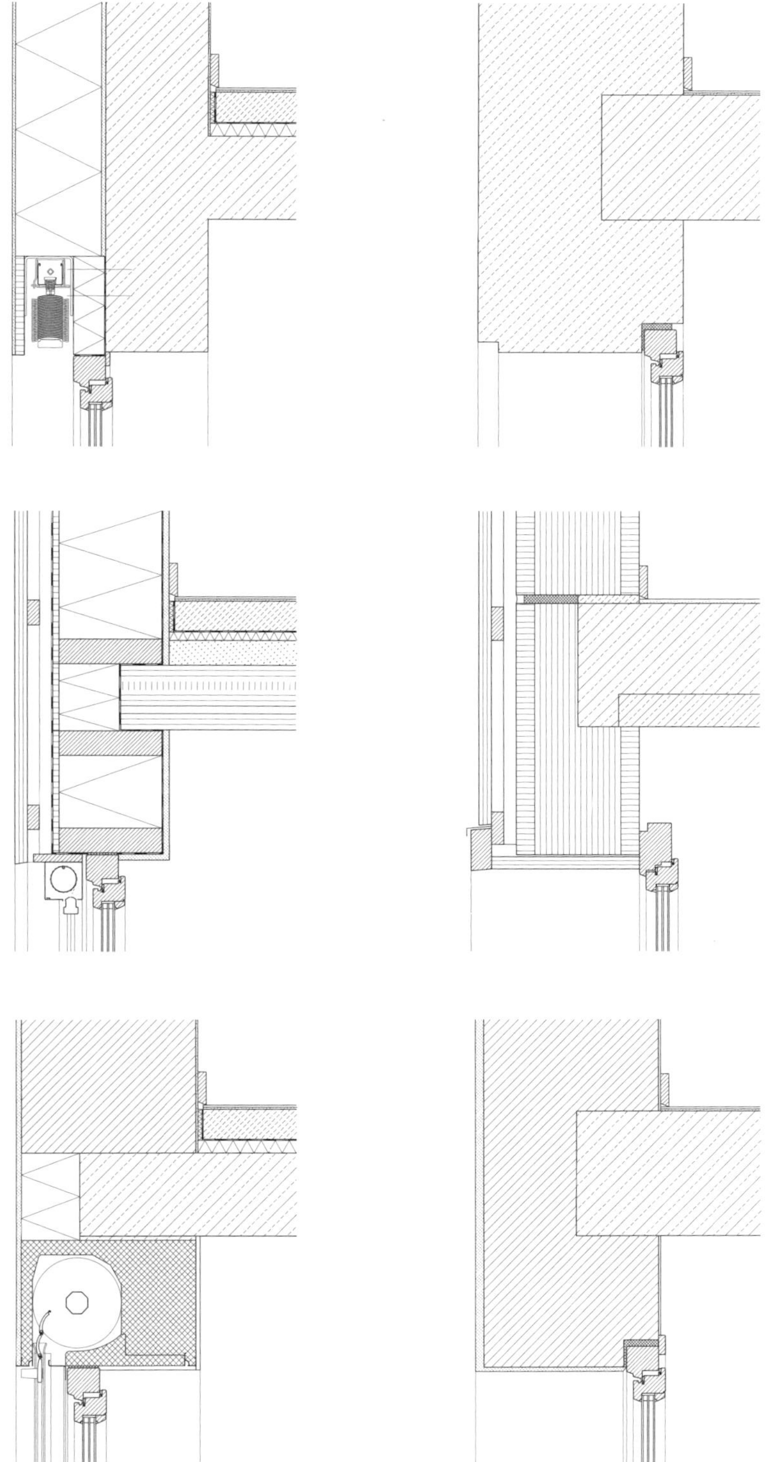

29
Comparison of standard wall construction with monolithic construction used in the research houses

The joints between the various building components, external wall, window lintel, and ceiling are shown in Figure 29. The standard construction details in use today are shown on the left. Shown opposite them on the right are the simple construction details developed and used for the research houses in Bad Aibling.

Special materials and a design that focuses on the properties of the materials allow this level of simplification. The various window forms arise from the specific possibilities of spanning the window opening offered by each material.

In the case of the facade in solid wood, the only possibility was a rectangular window opening because the loads are carried by the fibers in the wood. The infra-lightweight concrete wall is constructed without reinforcement. Designing the building around the properties of the material does away with the need for reinforcement. This made sense both economically and ecologically because, although steel may comprise only approximately 5–15 percent of the mass of reinforced concrete, it is responsible for a large part of its cost and environmental impact. Concrete is very strong in compression but weak in tension if not reinforced. A straight lintel without steel reinforcement would crack very quickly. The opening in this case therefore has a circular arch. In the masonry, it was also possible to do without steel-reinforced special components. The window opening here can also be spanned with a masonry segmental arch.

30
Various ways of forming the
window opening in the wall in
masonry, timber, and concrete

B7　Conclusion

It is possible to build buildings simply, to operate buildings simply, and conserve the environment over the whole life cycle of the building, all at the same time.
To do this, you must observe the following rules:

- Reduce the building envelope area.
  Increase building density.

- The window glass area should equal 10–15 percent of the room area to be lit.

- Use the thermal inertia of the building components for the indoor climate. Enable night ventilation.

- Use robust building services systems that consider users' behavior.

- Prepare for adaptations and modifications. Separate the technical services systems from the construction.

- Combine a small number of single-material component layers to form robust, durable constructions.

These strategies are not new—on the contrary, they have been known for ages. However, using them in a logical combination leads to a sustainable outcome. Therefore, not only policy-makers—for example, with decisions over building density—but also producers, planners, designers, and contractors should realign their actions with these guidelines.

Building the research houses was a good opportunity to build up practical experience in this field. For example, the preconditions for the intended building density of the three buildings had first to be established through a development plan procedure. The information exchange between the project stakeholders was more intensive and extensive than usual; for example, the nonstandard construction methods had first to be proposed and approved. Early communication of the strategy to all participants in the planning, design, and construction processes is essential to avoid misunderstandings and uncertainties and to resolve any concerns. This cooperation can pay off in the form of worthwhile improvements, for example, the simplification of timber construction details. The concept has attracted a lot of interest from planners, designers, clients, and trades organizations.

The results are presented in the form of performance parameters, drawings, and photos of the research houses in Part C of this guide.

31

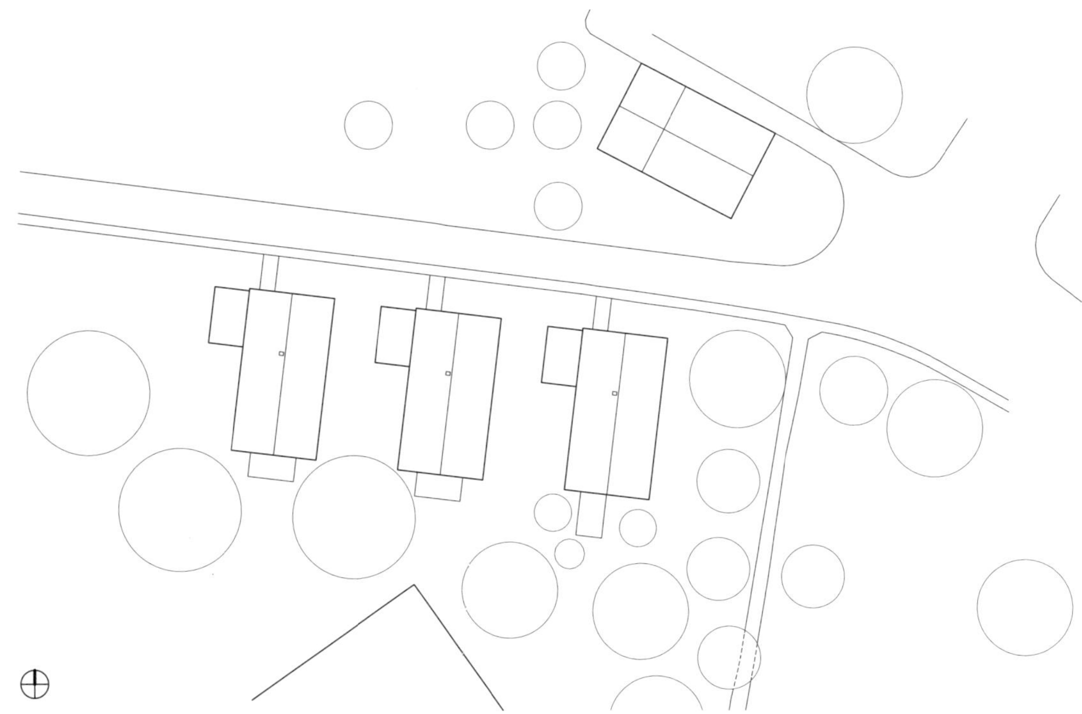

Client: B&O Group

Architect: Florian Nagler Architekten

Consultant: Forschungszentrum Einfach Bauen,
Technical University of Munich

Structural engineering: merz kley partner

Energy: Transsolar KlimaEngineering

Building physics: Horstmann + Berger

Fire protection: PHIplan

33
Site plan
scale 1:1000

Parameters of the infra-lightweight concrete building

Gross floor area (GFA):	648 m²
Building costs + technology excluding VAT:	€ 1,321,000
Cost index building + technology excluding VAT / GFA:	€ 2,039
Global warming potential building (GWP)[1]:	4.00 $kgCO_2e/m^2a$
Nonrenewable primary energy building (PENRE)[1]:	10.61 kWh/m^2a
Primary energy demand of heating and hot water preparation, calculated (QP)[2]:	31.27 kWh/m^2a
CO_2 emissions by heating and hot water preparation, calculated[2]:	18.14 kg/m^2a

Parameters of the solid wood building

Gross floor area (GFA):	648 m²
Building costs + technology excluding VAT:	€ 1,121,000
Cost index building + technology excluding VAT / GFA:	€ 1,730
Global warming potential building (GWP)[1]:	3.39 $kgCO_2e/m^2a$
Nonrenewable primary energy building (PENRE)[1]:	10.01 kWh/m^2a
Primary energy demand of heating and hot water preparation, calculated (QP)[2]:	30.48 kWh/m^2a
CO_2 emissions by heating and hot water preparation, calculated[2]:	17.67 kg/m^2a

Parameters of the masonry building

Gross floor area (GFA):   648 m^2

Building costs + technology excluding VAT: € 968,000

Cost index building + technology excluding VAT/GFA: € 1,493

Global warming potential building (GWP)[1]:   3.93 kgCO$_2$e/m^{2}a

Non-renewable primary energy building (PENRE)[1]:   11.12 kWh/m^{2}a

Primary energy demand of heating and hot water preparation,
calculated (QP)[2]:   31.37 kWh/m^{2}a

CO_2 emissions by heating and hot water preparation,
calculated[2]:   18.20 kg/m^{2}a

[1] Components considered: floor slab, external walls, windows, ceilings, internal walls, and roof; observed life cycle 100 years, manufacture (A1–A3), replacement (B4) and disposal (C1–C4); observation period 100 years; reference floor area is the usable floor area; assessment method ÖKOBAUDAT 2019-III (May 29, 2019); method: DIN EN ISO 14040 and DIN EN ISO 14044, DIN EN 15978, DIN EN 15804; sources: Research report "Einfach Bauen 2—Planen, Bauen, Messen; Anwendung integraler Strategien für energieeffizientes, einfaches Bauen mit Holz, Leichtbeton und hochwärmedämmendem Mauerwerk in Pilotprojekten anhand der Ergebnisse aus SWD-10.08.18.7-16.29"

[2] Calculated values; sources: Verification for a residential building in accordance with the German Energy Conservation Regulations (EnEV) 2016

C1   Infra-Lightweight Concrete Building

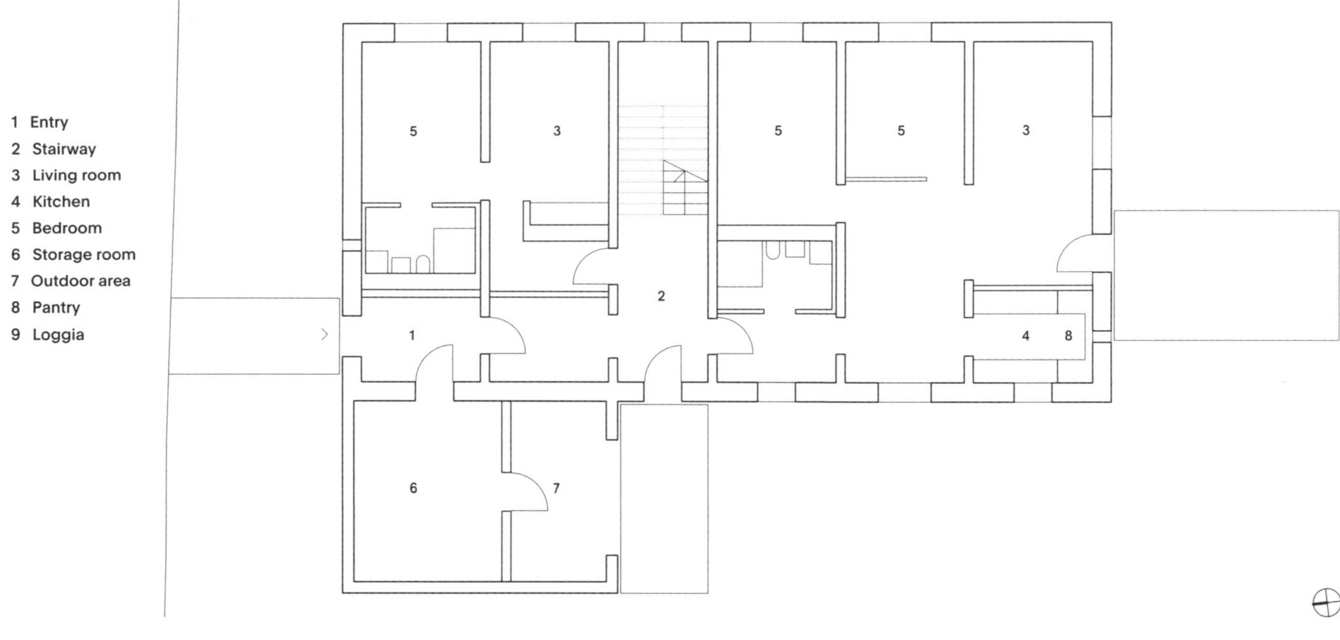

C1   64   34

35
Floor plan
ground floor
scale 1:200

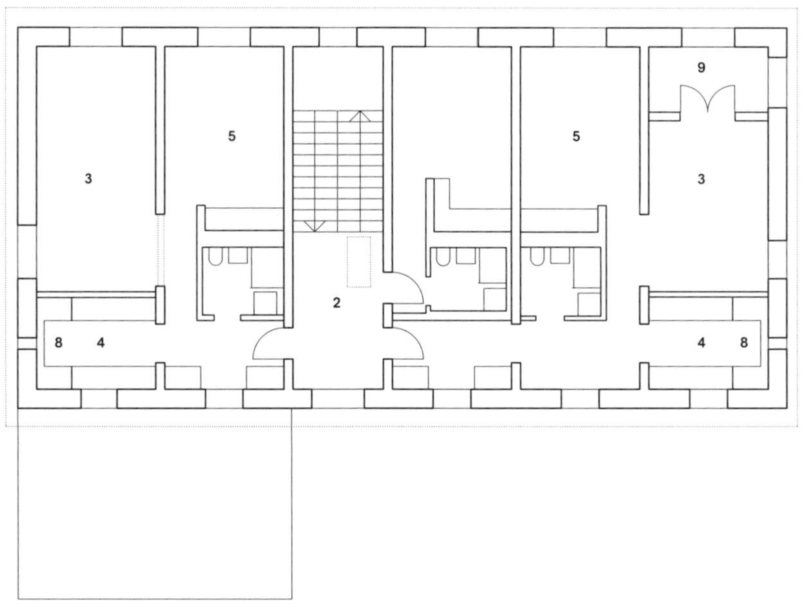

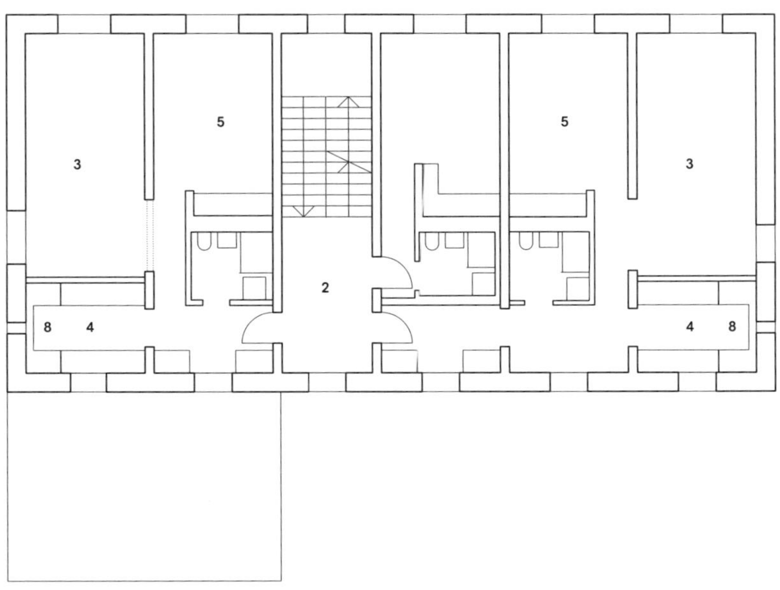

36
Floor plan
second floor
scale 1:200

37
Floor plan
first floor
scale 1:200

Infra-Lightweight Concrete Building

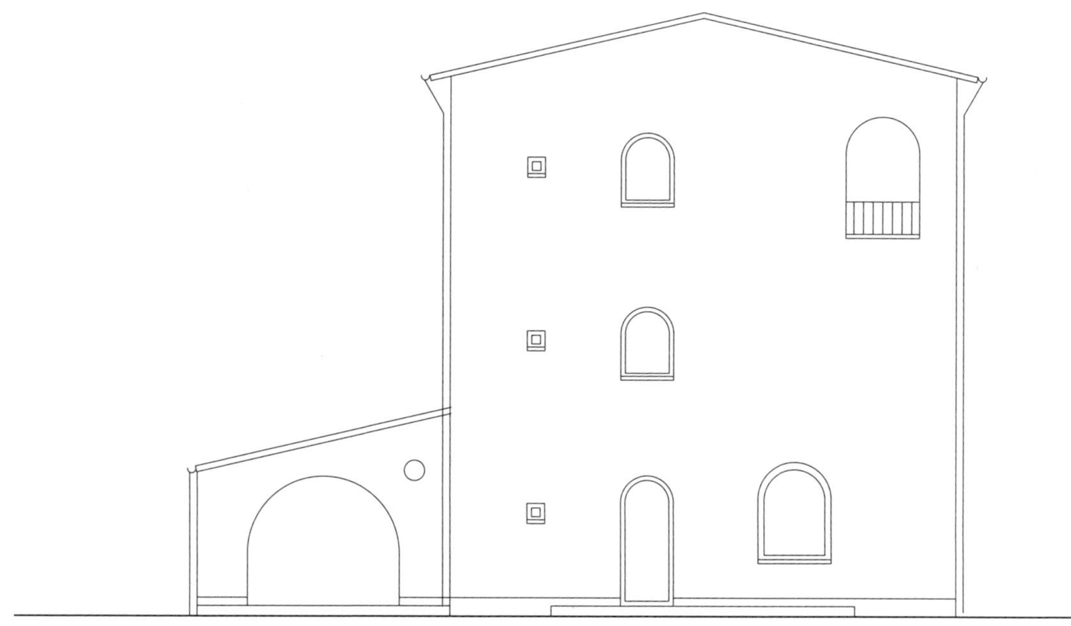

39
South elevation
Scale 1:200

40
East elevation
Scale 1:200

C1   68   41

Infra-Lightweight Concrete Building

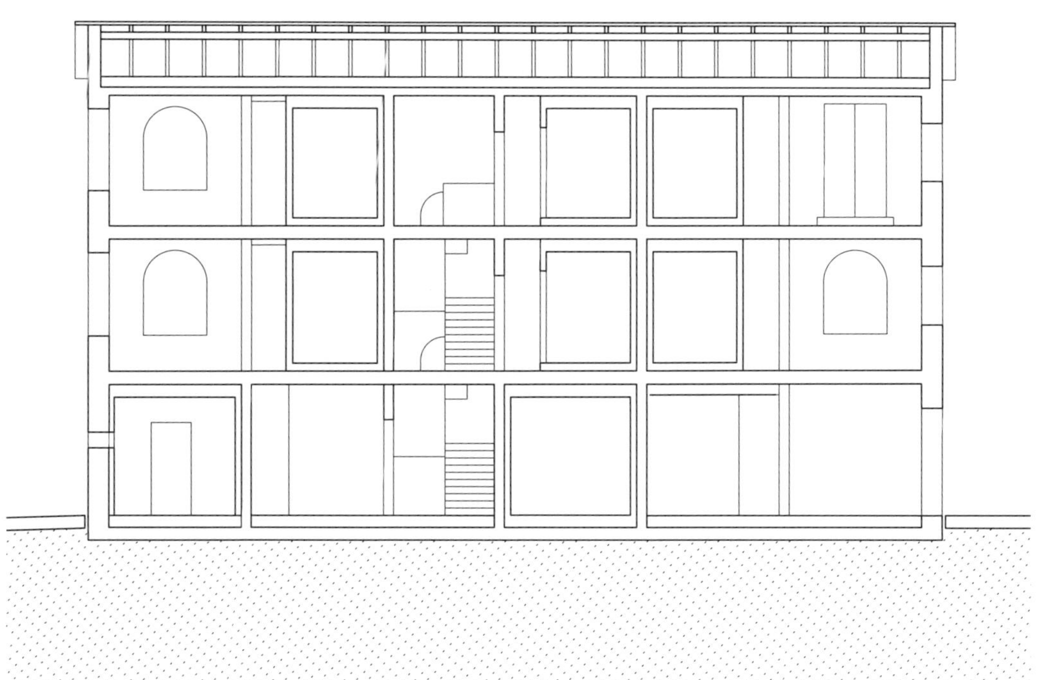

69

42
Cross section
Scale 1:200

43
Longitudinal section
Scale 1:200

C1   70   44

Infra-Lightweight Concrete Building

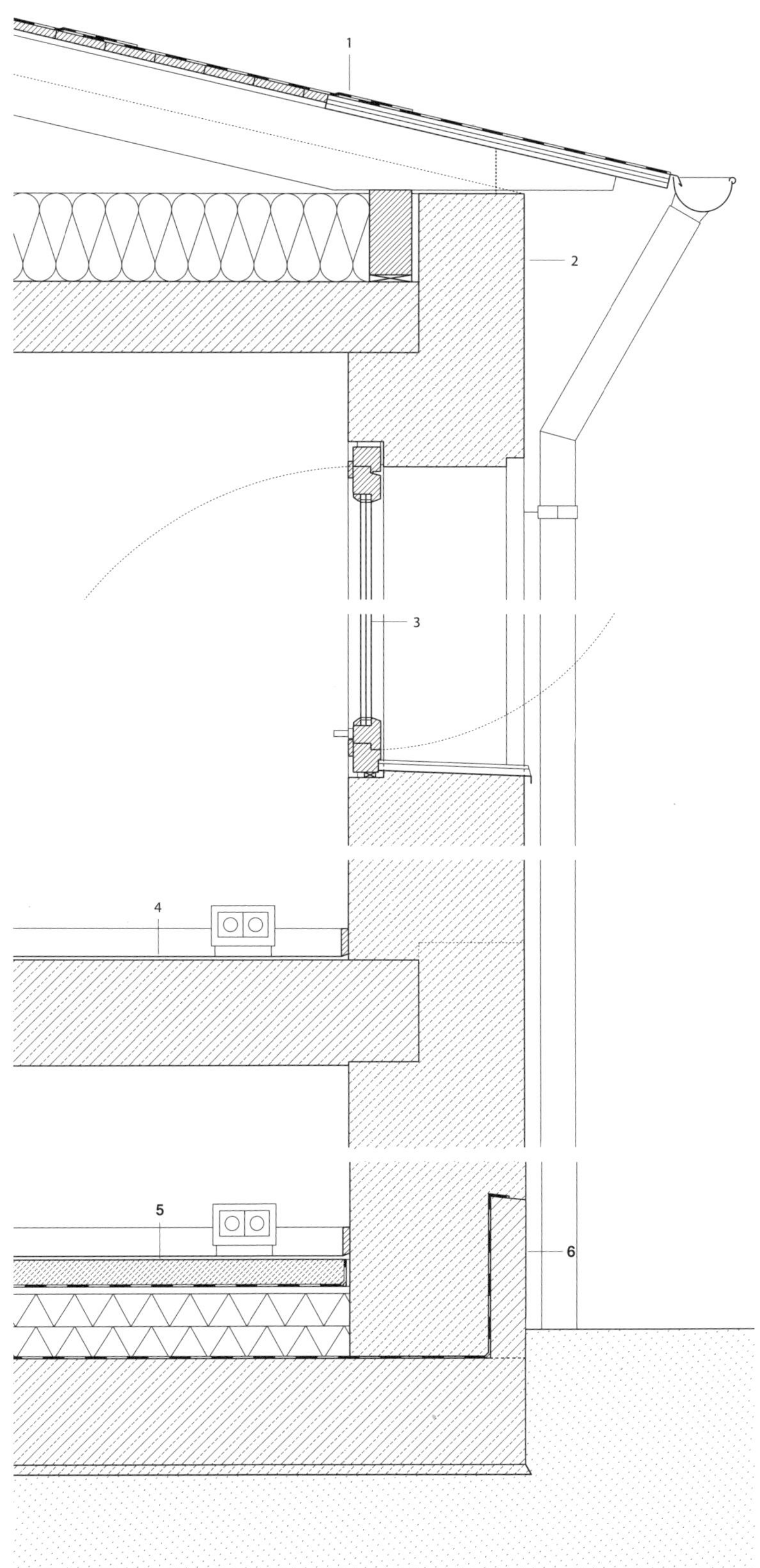

1   Bituminous membrane sanded
    23 mm wood decking,
    40 mm 3-ply CLT board in edge area
    80/220 rafters
    240 mm wood fiber insulation
    200 mm steel-fiber reinforced concrete
    U-value roof 0.16 W/m²K

2   500 mm infra-lightweight concrete,
    unreinforced
    U-value wall 0.357 W/m²K

3   Wood window, oiled, triple-glazed
    U-value window 0.9 W/m²K

4   Floor covering, impact sound reduction
    index ≥ 18 dB
    300 mm steel-fiber reinforced concrete

5   Floor covering, 75 mm cement screed
    separating layer
    20 mm mineral wool
    180 mm wood fiber insulation
    bituminous membrane
    300 mm reinforced concrete
    50 mm blinding layer, substrate founded
    on frost-free and compacted material
    U-value floor slab 0.197 W/m²K

6   Reinforced concrete upstand,
    protection for waterproofing, 100 mm
    bituminous membrane

45
Facade section
Scale 1:20

Infra-Lightweight Concrete Building

Infra-Lightweight Concrete Building

C1 76 50

Infra-Lightweight Concrete Building

Infra-Lightweight Concrete Building

C1   80   54

Infra-Lightweight Concrete Building

C2   Solid Wood Building

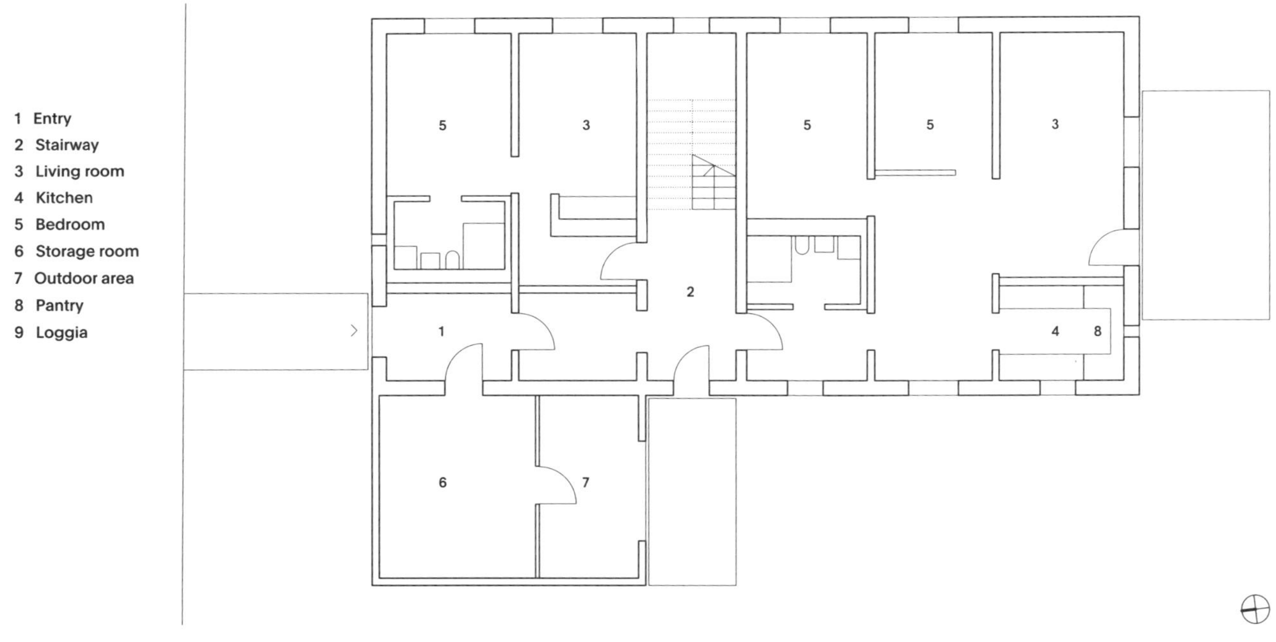

56
Floor plan
ground floor
scale 1:200

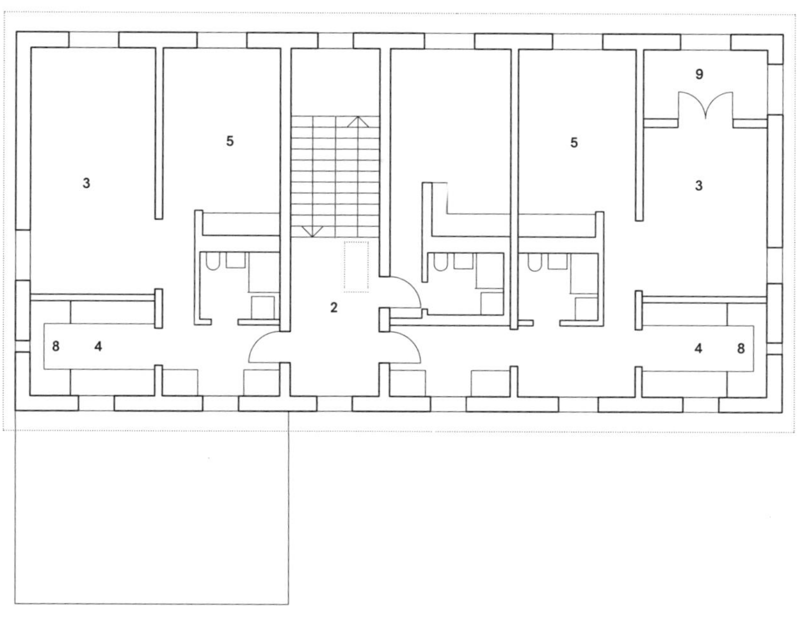

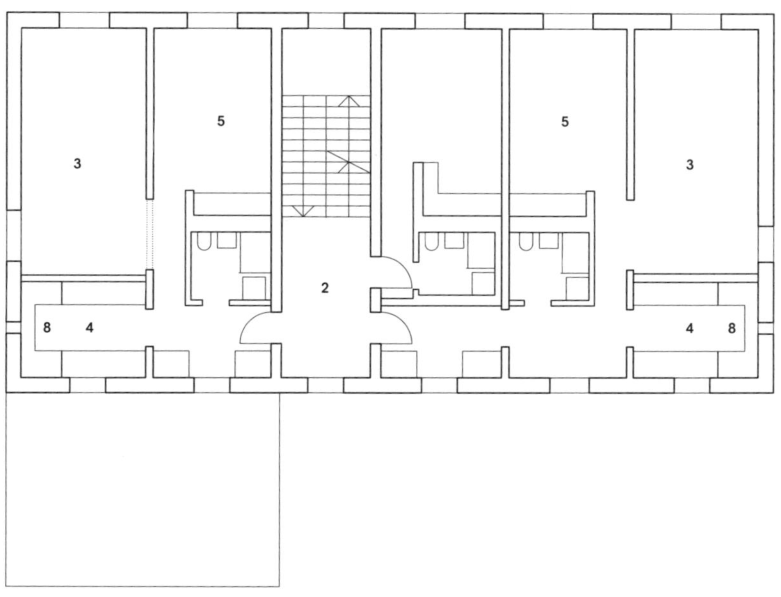

57
Floor plan
second floor
scale 1:200

58
Floor plan
first floor
scale 1:200

C2   84   59

Solid Wood Building

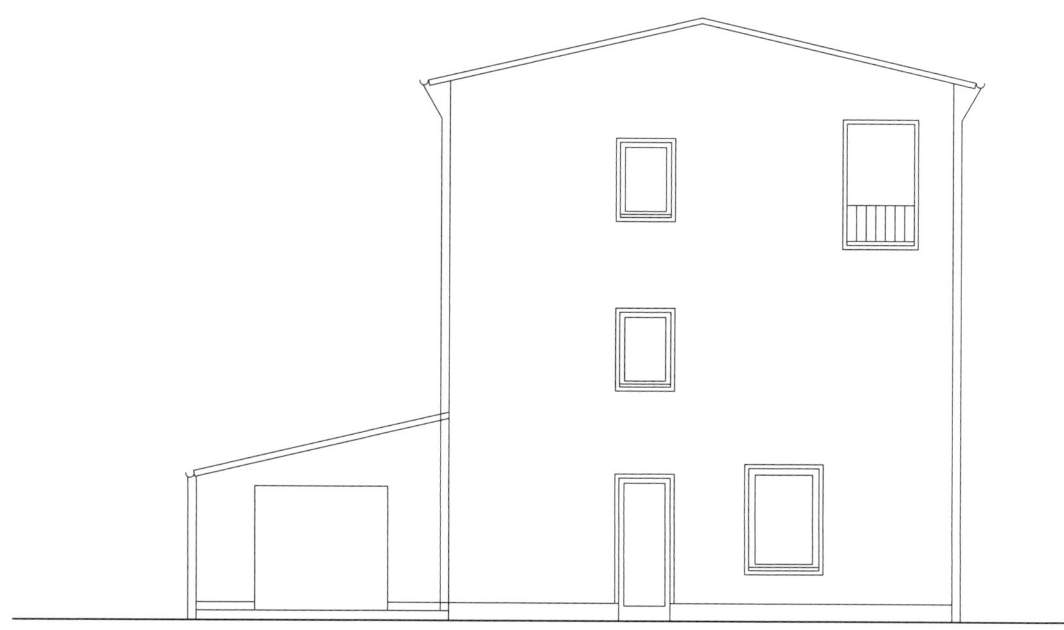

60
South elevation
scale 1:200

61
East elevation
scale 1:200

C2   86   62

Solid Wood Building

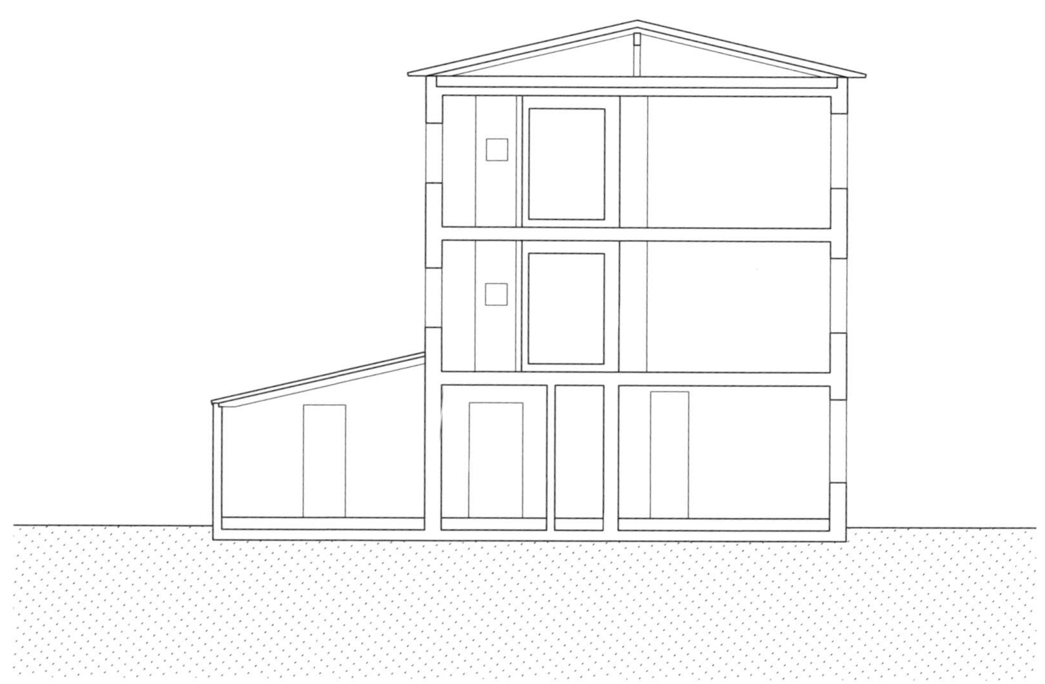

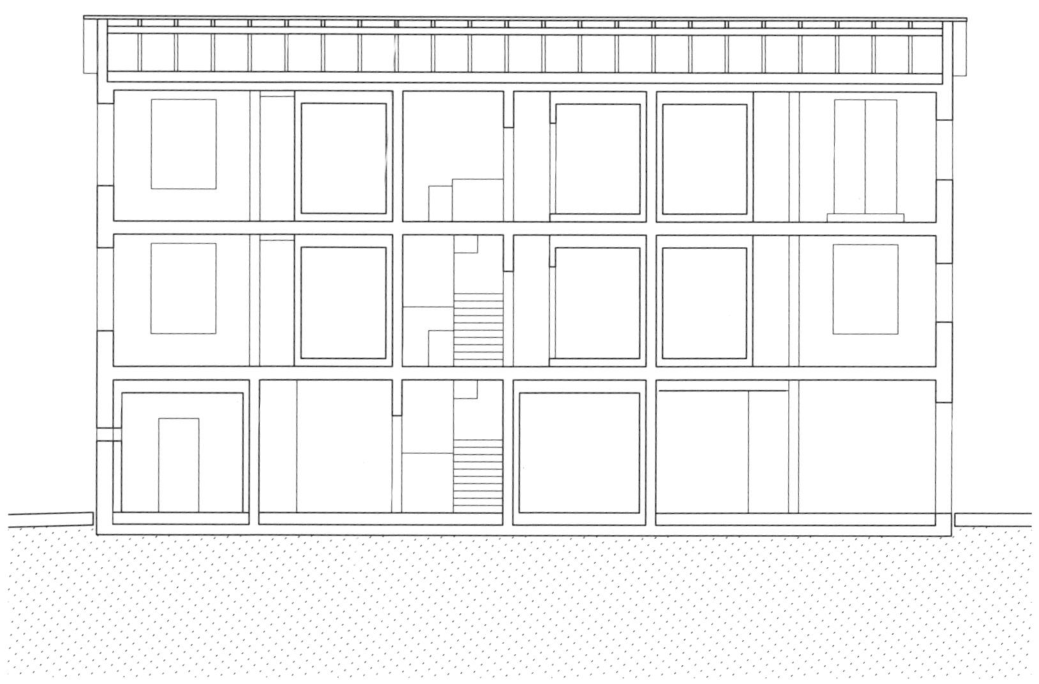

63
Cross section
scale 1:200

64
Longitudinal section
scale 1:200

C2   88   65

Solid Wood Building

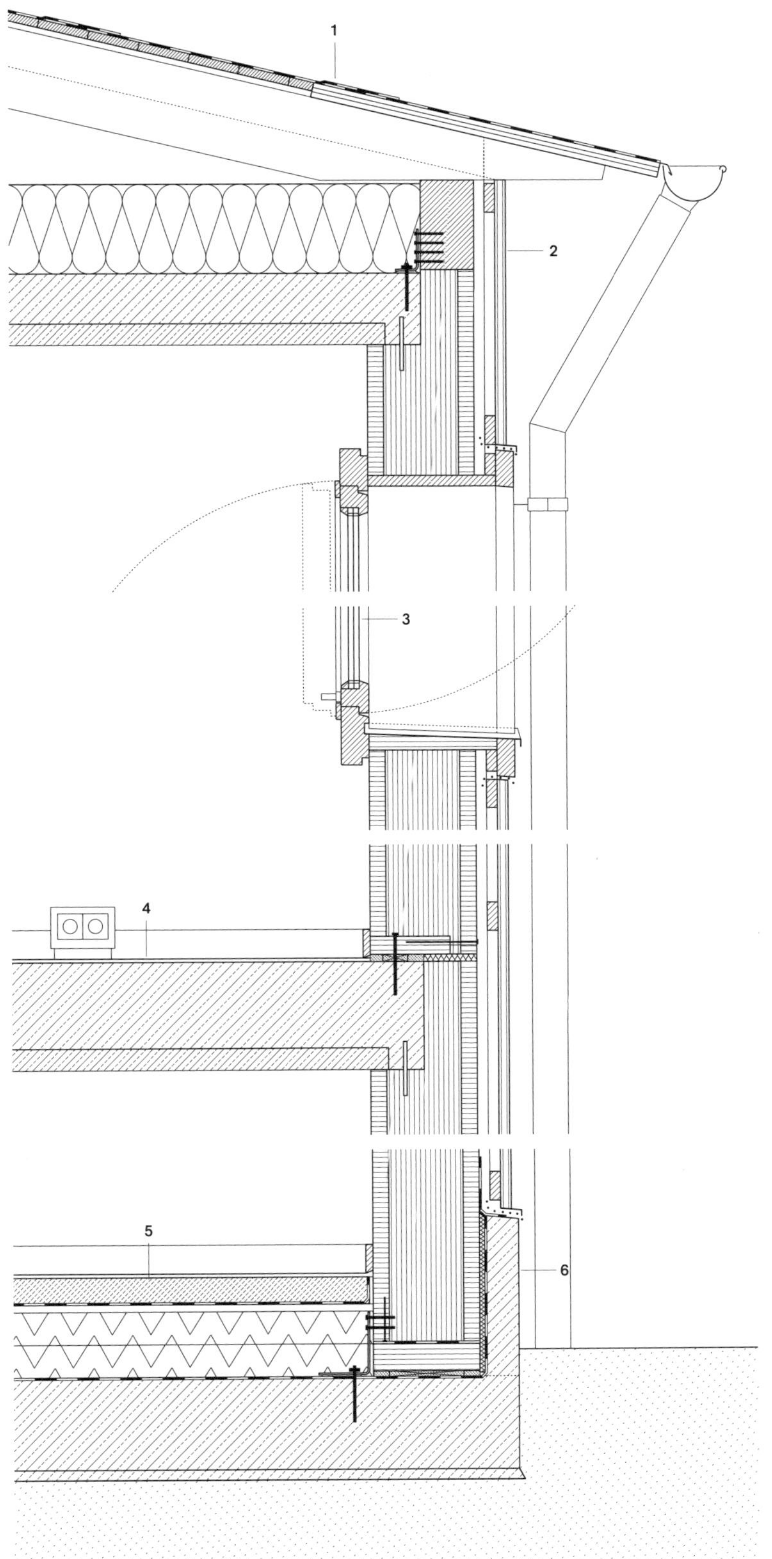

1   Bituminous membrane sanded
     23 mm wood decking,
     40 mm 3-ply CLT board in edge area
     80/220 rafters
     240 mm wood fiber insulation
     200 mm reinforced concrete
     precast unit with concrete topping
     U-value roof 0.16 W/m²K

2   Pine cladding, rough sawn
     tile battens
     counter battens
     solid timber wall 300 mm, with air voids
     U-value wall 0.224 W/m²K

3   Wood window, oiled, triple-glazed
     U-value window 0.9 W/m²K

4   Floor covering, impact sound reduction
     index ≥ 18 dB
     300 mm reinforced concrete,
     precast unit with concrete topping

5   Floor covering, 75 mm cement screed
     separating layer
     20 mm mineral wool
     180 mm wood fiber insulation
     bituminous membrane
     300 mm reinforced concrete
     50 mm blinding layer, substrate founded
     on frost-free and compacted material
     U-value floor slab 0.197 W/m²K

6   Reinforced concrete upstand,
     protection for waterproofing, 100 mm
     bituminous membrane

66
Facade section
scale 1:20

C2   90   67

Solid Wood Building

91   68

C2   92   69

Solid Wood Building

C2   94   70

Solid Wood Building

95   71

C2   96   72

Solid Wood Building

C2   98   73

Solid Wood Building

C2   100   75

Solid Wood Building

C3   Thermally Insulating Masonry Building

1 Entry
2 Stairway
3 Living room
4 Kitchen
5 Bedroom
6 Storage room
7 Outdoor area
8 Pantry
9 Loggia
10 Building services

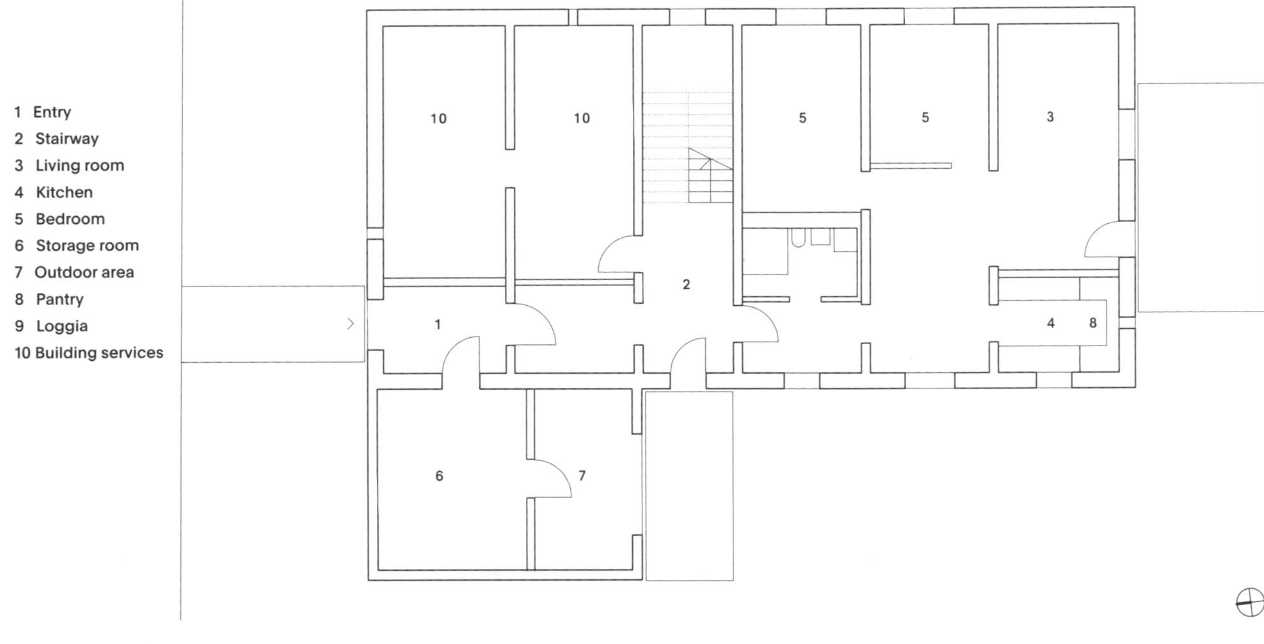

77
Floor plan
ground floor
scale 1:200

Thermally Insulating Masonry Building

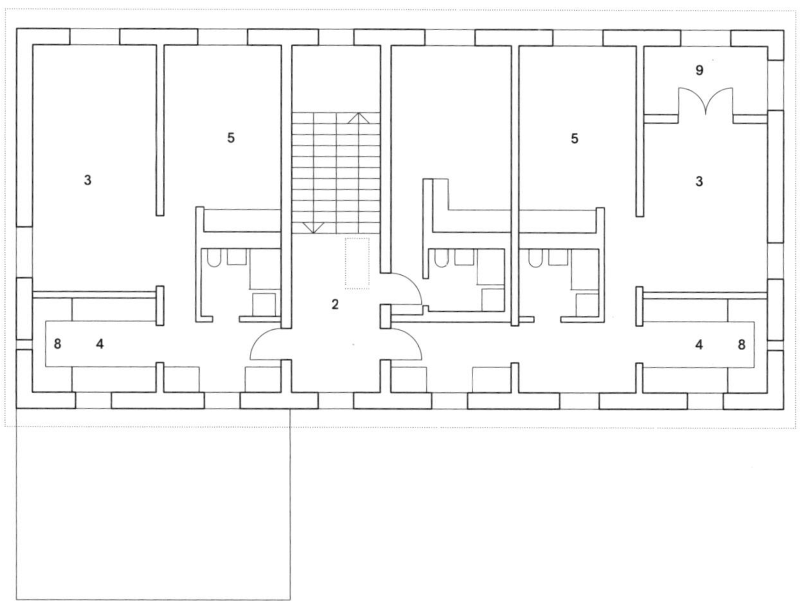

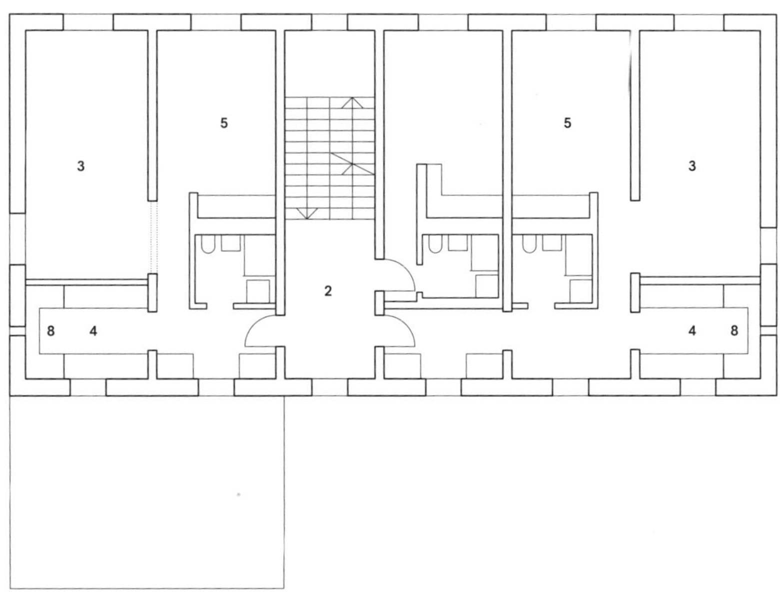

78
Floor plan
second floor
scale 1:200

79
Floor plan
first floor
scale 1:200

Thermally Insulating Masonry Building

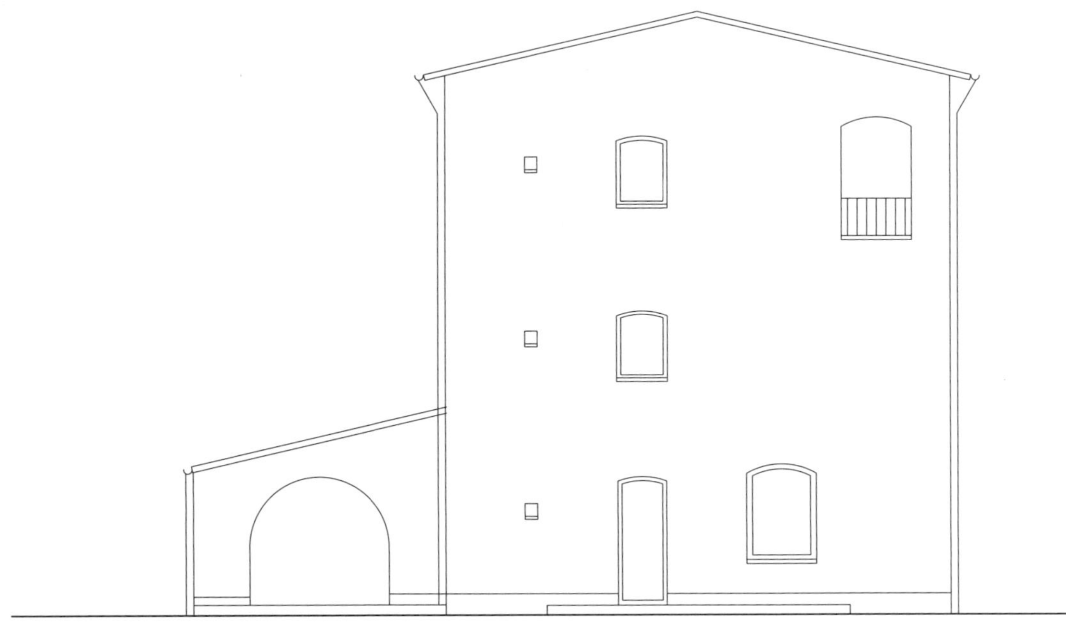

105

81
South elevation
scale 1:200

82
East elevation
scale 1:200

Thermally Insulating Masonry Building

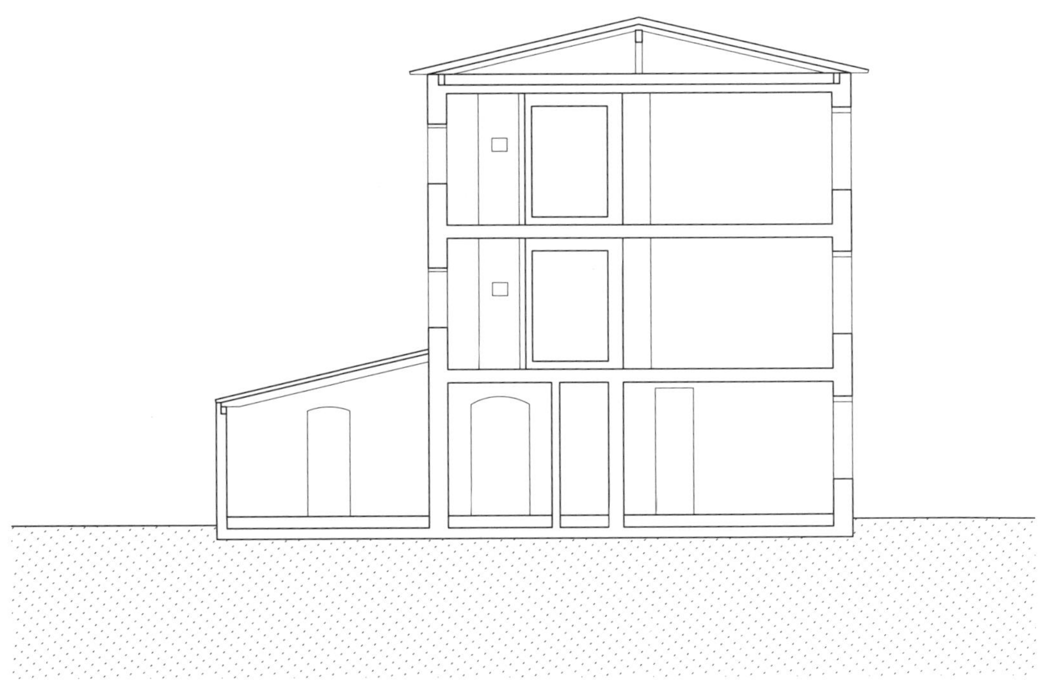

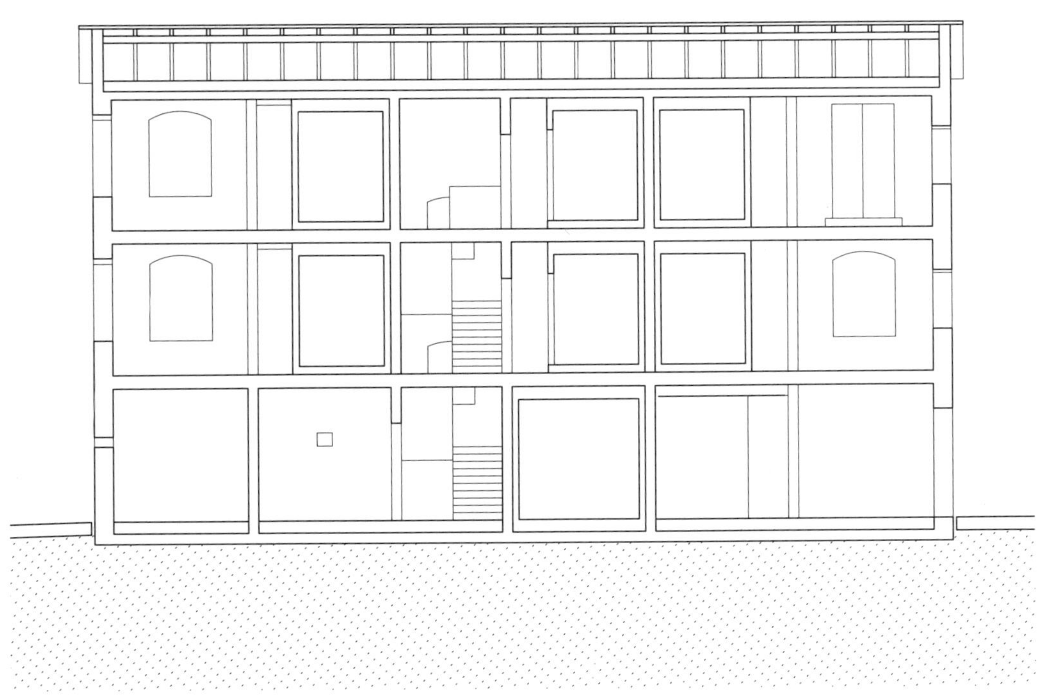

84
Cross section
scale 1:200

85
Longitudinal section
scale 1:200

C3 108 86

Thermally Insulating Masonry Building

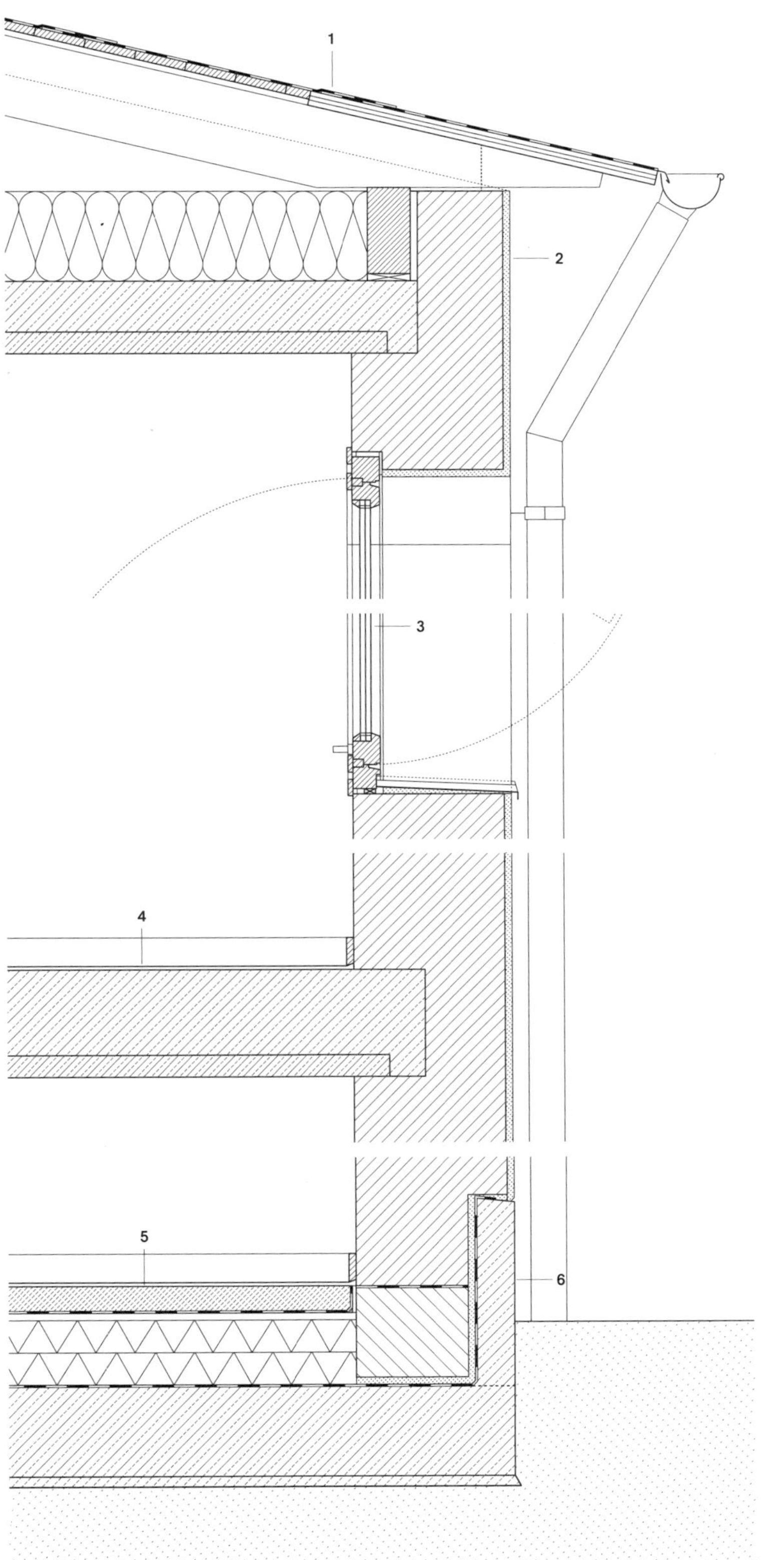

1 Bituminous membrane sanded
23 mm wood decking,
40 mm 3-ply CLT board in edge area
80/220 rafters
240 mm wood fiber insulation
200 mm reinforced concrete
precast unit with concrete topping
U-value roof 0.16 W/m²K

2 Lime-cement lightweight rendering
mortar 20 mm, 1-layer,
no fabric reinforcing mesh
420 mm hollow clay masonry unit
5 mm lime slurry
U-value wall 0.248 W/m²K

3 Wood window, oiled, triple-glazed
U-value window 0.9 W/m²K

4 Floor covering, impact sound reduction
index ≥ 18 dB
300 mm reinforced concrete,
precast unit with concrete topping

5 Floor covering, 75 mm cement screed
separating layer
20 mm mineral wool
180 mm wood fiber insulation
bituminous membrane
300 mm reinforced concrete

6 Reinforced concrete upstand,
protection for waterproofing, 100 mm
bituminous membrane

87
Facade section
scale 1:20

Thermally Insulating Masonry Building

Thermally Insulating Masonry Building

C3   114   92

Thermally Insulating Masonry Building

Thermally Insulating Masonry Building

117   95

Thermally Insulating Masonry Building

C3   120   97

Thermally Insulating Masonry Building

D Literature

Part A

[1] Baukostensenkungskommission (BKSK). Bericht der Baukostensenkungskommission des Bündnisses für bezahlbares Wohnen
und Bauen. Berlin: Bundesministerium für Umwelt, Naturschutz,
Bau und Reaktorsicherheit (BUNBR), 2015.

[2] Auer, Thomas. "Simple Building. XIA – Intelligente Architektur"
(2014): 10–12.

[3] GEWOFAG 2016: Forschungsprojekt Riem. https://www.
gewofag.de/web.nsf/id/8-seiter-forschungshauser-riem-
gewofag/$file/8-Seiter_Forschungshaeuser_Riem.pdf
(accessed April 6, 2020).

[4] Höhne, Valerie, Alexander Neubacher, and Gerald Traufetter.
"Störfaktor Mensch." Der Spiegel (July 2017). https://magazin.
spiegel.de/SP/2017/7/149533943/index.html
(accessed February 14, 2017).

[5] Eberle, Dietmar, and Florian Aicher, eds. be 2226: Die
Temperatur der Architektur/The Temperature of Architecture.
Basel: Birkhäuser, 2016.

[6] Nagler, Florian, et al. Einfach Bauen: Ganzheitliche Strategien für
energieeffizientes, einfaches Bauen: Untersuchung der
Wechselwirkung von Raum, Technik, Material und Konstruktion.
Stuttgart: Fraunhofer IRB Verlag, 2019.

[7] The European Parliament and the Council of the European
Union. Regulation (EU) No. 305/2011 of the European Parliament
and of the Council, Annex I, March 9, 2011. https://www.
ce-richtlinien.eu/alles/richtlinien/Bauprodukte/Richtlinie/
Bauprodukteverordnung_EU_305_2011.pdf
(accessed May 28, 2020).

[8] DIN EN 15804:2020-03: Sustainability of Construction Works—
Environmental Product Declarations—Core Rules for the Product
Category of Construction Products. Berlin: Beuth, March 2020.

[9] König, Holger, Nikolaus Kohler, Johannes Kreißig, and Thomas
Lützkendorf, eds. A Life Cycle Approach to Buildings: Principles,
Calculations, Design Tools. Munich: Detail, 2010.

Literature

[10]   Bundesinstitut für Bau-, Stadt- und Raumforschung (BBSR). ÖKOBAUDAT 2019-III. Berlin: Federal Ministry of the Interior, Building and Community, 2019. https://www.oekobaudat.de/en/database/archive/oekobaudat-2019-iii.html (accessed May 3, 2019, last updated on May 29, 2019).

[11] & [12] Umweltbundesamt. "Flugreisen," esp. Table 1: Treibhausgasemissionen beispielhafter Flüge. Umweltbundesamt. https://www.umweltbundesamt.de/ umwelttipps-fuer-den-alltag/mobilitaet/flugreisen (accessed April 28, 2020, last updated on April 9, 2019).

[13]   See [9].

[14]   DIN ISO 14044:2009-11: Environmental Management. Berlin: Beuth, November 2009.

[15]   See [9].

[16]   DIN EN ISO 14025:2011-10: Environmental Labels and Declarations—Type III Environmental Declarations—Principles and Procedures. Berlin: Beuth, October 2011.

[17]   DIN EN 15978:2012-10: Sustainability of Construction Works—Assessment of Environmental Performance of Buildings—Calculation Method. Berlin: Beuth, October 2012.

Part B

[18]   BKI. Baukosten 2020 Neubau, part 1, Statistische Kostenkennwerte für Gebäude. Stuttgart: BKI, 2020.

[19]   DIN V 4108-6:2003-06. Thermal Protection and Energy Economy in Buildings— Part 6: Calculation of Annual Heat and Energy Use. Berlin: Beuth, June 2003.

[20]   Keller, Bruno, and Stephan Rutz. Pinpoint: Fakten der Bauphysik zu nach- haltigem Bauen. 2nd ed. Zürich: vdf Hochschulverlag AG at the ETH Zürich, 2011.

[21]   See [5].

[22]   See [20].

[23]   Knecht, Kevin, and Diego Sigrist. Vergleich der beiden Lüftungskonzepte der Siedlung Klee bezüglich Ökologie und Ökonomie sowie Befragung der Bewohner. Dübendorf: s3 GmbH, 2019.

[24]   Delzendeh, Elham, Song Wu, Angela Lee, and Ying Zhou. "The Impact of Occupants' Behaviours on Building Energy Analysis: A Research Review." Renewable and Sustainable Energy Reviews 80 (December 2017): 1061–71.

[25] Oberste Baubehörde im Bayerischen Staatsministerium des Innern. e% – Energieeffizienter Wohnungsbau: Planungshinweise für den Wohnungsbau. Munich: OBB, 2010. https://www.ar.tum.de/fileadmin/w00bfl/klima/Publikationen/Berichte/Veroeffentlichung_Planungshilfen_OBB.pdf (accessed June 2, 2021).

[26] Schneider, Birgit. "Nutzerverhalten bei Sanierungen berücksichtigen." BINE Informationsdienst: Projektinfo 02/2015: Energieforschung konkret. Aachen: E.ON Energy Research Center at RWTH Aachen University, 2015.

[27] IWU. "Berücksichtigung des Nutzerverhaltens bei energetischen Verbesserungen. Institut für Wohnen und Umwelt GmbH (IWU)." BBSR-Online-Publikation (April 2019). https://www.iwu.de/research/energie/2016/nutzerverhalten-bei-energetischen-verbesserungen/ (accessed June 2, 2021).

[28] DIN V 4108-6.

[29] 4701-10.

[30] 18599.

[31] Tam, Vivian W. Y., Laura Almeida, and Khoa Le. "Energy-Related Occupant Behaviour and Its Implications in Energy Use: A Chronological Review." Sustainability 10, no. 8 (2018): 2635.

[32] Brager, Gail S., and Richard de Dear. "Climate, Comfort, and Natural Ventilation: A New Adaptive Comfort Standard for ASHRAE Standard 55." Proceedings, Moving Thermal Comfort Standards into the 21st Century, Windsor, UK, April 5–8, 2001. Windsor: Oxford Brookes University, 2001.

[33] Ruhnau, Dagmar. "Auf dem richtigen Weg – Aktivplus-Studentenwohnhaus 'Campo V' in Stuttgart." db Deutsche Bauzeitung 154, no. 5 (2020): 52–55.

[34] GEWOFAG. Riem, 2014. See [3].

[35] Brand, Stewart. How Buildings Learn: What Happens After They're Built. New York: Penguin, 1994.

[36] Ritter, Frank. "Lebensdauer von Bauteilen und Bauelementen." In BKI Baukosten 2019 Neubau, Part 2, Statistische Kostenkennwerte für Bauelemente. Stuttgart: BKI Baukosteninformationszentrum, 2019.

[37] Schlaich, Mike, and El Zareef, Mohamed Ahmed Mohamed. "Infraleichtbeton." Beton- und Stahlbetonbau 103, no. 3 (2008): 175–82.

[38] Schlaich, Mike, and Alex Hückler. "Infraleichtbeton 2.0." Beton- und Stahlbetonbau 107, no. 11 (2012): 757–66.

Literature